# OUR KINGDOM STANDS ON BRITTLE GLASS

Papers from
Mental Health Education and Practice for
Chicanos and the Mexican American Community:
A "State of the Art" Workshop
April 1-3, 1981, San Antonio, Texas

*Guadalupe Gibson,*
*Editor*

 National Association of Social Workers
Silver Spring, Maryland

Publication of this volume was made possible in part by a grant
from the National Institute of Mental Health.


Library of Congress Cataloging in Publication Data

Main entry under title:

Our kingdom stands on brittle glass.

  Includes bibliographical references.
  1. Mexican Americans—Mental health services—
Congresses. 2. Mental health education—United
States—Congresses. 3. Social work with minorities—
United States—Congresses. 4. Mexican Americans—
Services for—Congresses. I. Gibson, Guadalupe.
RC451.5.M4809 1982      362.2'08968073      82-22532
ISBN 0-87101-199-0


Printed in U.S.A.

# *Foreword*

*T*he educators and practitioners who attended the "State of the Art" Workshop at the Worden School of Social Service in San Antonio, Texas, met to discuss their perceptions of current mental health education and practice among Chicanos. They succeeded in doing much more. At the workshop, this highly cohesive group of Chicanos set out with clarity of purpose and a strong sense of determination to achieve what is important to them and to their people, one of their objectives being to develop models of practice that would influence traditional models. In doing so, they have provided impetus and direction for social workers who are Chicanos and have raised some dramatic questions for the rest of us: What does it mean to be a Chicano or Chicana and a social worker? What is the importance of ideology? For that matter, what is social work's ideology? Most basic, is social work's agenda the same as that of social workers who are Chicanos?

The underlying theme of the work of the group as presented in the workshop papers is that the culture of individuals—clients and workers alike—is an absolutely fundamental and integral part of their personal identity. The recurrent question addressed is, How can a recognition of this be made to permeate social work practice? Failure in this area would be a great failure indeed, for this issue goes to the heart of how well the profession serves its clients and workers.

We believe that *Our Kingdom Stands on Brittle Glass* contains information on the culture of Chicanos and social work practice with Chicanos that should be shared with social work educators and practitioners to the greatest possible extent. We hope by its publication and distribution to prompt the consideration of the fundamental questions raised and to extend further the knowledge developed in an important mental health project. The National Association of Social Workers is very pleased to be publishing this book.

MARY ANN QUARANTA, *President,*
*National Association of Social Workers*
ROBERT P. STEWART, *President-elect,*
*National Association of Social Workers*

*October 1982*

S072239

iii

# Table of Contents

## Summation

## *Additional Papers*

## *Glossary*

# Contributors

(*Positions are those held at the time of the workshop*)

**Tomás Atencio,** MSW, Doctoral Candidate, Department of Sociology, University of New Mexico, Albuquerque.

**Norma Benavides,** MSW, Field Specialist, University of Texas at Arlington.

**Ronald C. Bounous,** Ph.D., Professor, School of Social Work, University of Texas at Austin.

**Ismael Dieppa,** DSW, Dean, School of Social Work, Arizona State University, Tempe.

**Joseph S. Gallegos,** Ph.D., Coordinator, Multi-Ethnic Mental Health Training Project, School of Social Work, University of Washington, Seattle.

**Eunice C. Garcia,** MSSW, Specialist, School of Social Work, University of Texas at Austin.

**Guadalupe Gibson,** MSW, Associate Professor and Director, La Chicana and Mental Health Project, Worden School of Social Service, Our Lady of the Lake University of San Antonio, San Antonio, Texas.

**Ernesto Gomez,** Ph.D., Assistant Professor, Worden School of Social Service, Our Lady of the Lake University of San Antonio, San Antonio, Texas.

**Alvin O. Korte,** Ph.D., Associate Professor, Department of Social Work, New Mexico Highlands University, Las Vegas.

**Josie Torralba Romero,** MSW, South County Center Director, Santa Clara County Mental Health Bureau, Gilroy, California.

**Javier Saenz,** Ph.D., Unit Manager, Adult Day Treatment Unit, Salt Lake County Division of Mental Health, Salt Lake City, Utah.

**Juliette S. Silva,** Ph.D., Professor, Graduate School of Social Work, University of Denver, Denver, Colorado.

**Federico Souflée, Jr.,** MSSW, Director, Chicano Training Center, Houston, Texas.

**Albert Vazquez,** MSW, Executive Director, Pilsen-Little Village Community Mental Health Center, Chicago, Illinois.

# *Preface*

*T*he participants in the "State of the Art" Workshop held April 1-3, 1981 in San Antonio, Texas, at the Worden School of Social Service, Our Lady of the Lake University, considered it a landmark event.[1] It brought together Chicano and Chicana educators and practitioners who, it had become evident, had moved beyond rhetoric to paradigms. These professionals had put their ideas in writing and examined them critically and at the end of the three days of the workshop expressed a commitment to continue the work that had just begun.

The purpose of the workshop was to convene educators and practitioners who were providing mental health services to Chicanos and offer them an opportunity to discuss their perception of the "state of the art" of social work education and practice. We who planned the workshop felt that the time to assess the state of the art had come, for a decade of specially funded programs focusing on social work and mental health practice with Chicanos had recently ended. Largely because of the efforts of groups such as Trabajadores de la Raza, a coalition of Chicano and Chicana human service workers that by 1969 had become a national organization, many schools of social work and mental health centers had been receiving financial support for more than ten years from the National Institute of Mental Health. The aim behind this support was to develop interventive strategies for practice with Chicanos and to train students to practice with them in culturally relevant ways. However, little appeared to be known about the outcome of such projects. In addition, over the same period of time, the Council on Social Work Education, through Accreditation Standard 1234A, had been promoting the recruitment of minority students, including Chicanos, and requiring the inclusion of minority content in the curricula of schools of social work. It had also established a Commission on Minority Affairs. The National Association of Social Workers had set the eradication of poverty and racism as a priority and established a

---

[1] The workshop was made possible through an administrative extension grant to Grant #5 T01 MH14401-05 awarded to La Chicana and Mental Health Project, Worden School of Social Service, Our Lady of the Lake University of San Antonio, San Antonio, Texas, by the National Institute of Mental Health.

National Committee on Minority Affairs in 1975. But again, little was known of the impact that these developments were having among Chicanos. In light of this and the dwindling of resources and apparent retrenchment in services to minorities brought about by the current federal administration, it became imperative that we identify the state of the art in social work practice and education in relation to Chicanos.

Although general attention was to be paid to the trends in mental health education and practice over the past ten or twelve years, the "State of the Art" Workshop was to focus more specifically on practice models that had been developed during this period. Because funds through the grant that supported the workshop were limited, as were funds available to potential participants through their schools or programs, we found it necessary to restrict the emphasis of the workshop to the presentation of some models being developed and researched in academic settings and some being developed and tested out in the field, whether or not these had been fully evaluated. It was envisioned that a historical and ideological perspective would be presented to provide a framework within which to review the development of the models. We considered it essential to bring together systematically — to piece together — the developments of various educational programs as well as to cull out practice wisdom formulated in the field. Our profession, which developed mainly out of the experiences of practitioners, became scientific first by searching for empirical backing for its conclusions.[2] Practitioners continue to do the same as they see certain patterns develop in their practice. We wanted to emphasize the interdependence of education and practice in the development of culturally relevant models and in the preparation of students for practice, recognizing that "theory without practice is sterile, and practice without theory is blind."[3]

The professionals who were invited to make presentations at the workshop had been identified as individuals who had developed or were in the process of developing practice models. We were not only interested in knowing or learning about the application of the models but also about their conceptualization and the extent to which they had been empirically demonstrated to be effective in practice with Chicanos.

Model building is a complex task that may proceed inductively or deductively, theoretically or empirically. Models are visual, metaphoric

---

[2] Martin Loeb, "The Backdrop for Social Research: Theorymaking and Model Building." Unpublished manuscript, undated.

[3] See Ron Baker, "Notes on a Conceptual Framework for Unitary Social Work," *International Social Work*, 4 (1980), pp. 10-25.

representations of some part of reality and how it works.[4] They provide direction by serving as mechanisms for simplifying complex variables and showing deficiencies. Deutsch stated that models serve four functions: to organize, to explain and thus become heuristic, to predict, and to measure.[5] Perhaps because of this, model building is useful in testing theories and designing experiments.[6] The term "paradigm," which means an arrangement of central concepts, is often used interchangeably with the term "model." For our purpose, a model was thought to be a conceptual map or design, a table, a pattern, or an example that involves symbolizations and abstractions capable of being modified and readopted and that has been or is being tested or evaluated. When verified in propositional form, such a model can qualify as part of theory.[7]

Following our original plan, papers describing overviews and perspectives were the first presented at the workshop to set up a framework within which the practice models could be reviewed. Joseph Gallegos presented the historical perspective and Tomás Atencio the ideological one. Ronald Bounous offered a framework for the formulation of interventive theory that could be useful in the further development of models. When the models themselves were presented, each was subjected to scrutiny by a designated "reactor" and by the rest of the participants, an activity that was considered productive. At the end of the workshop, Ismael Dieppa presented a summary and analysis of the papers and indicated some directions for the continued endeavors of Chicano and Chicana practitioners and educators, giving particular emphasis to prevention and to health promotion.

Because of the limitations of time, the number of participants who were asked to present papers over the three days of the workshop was relatively small. Nevertheless, we encouraged everyone invited to San Antonio to submit papers that could be considered for inclusion in any subsequent publication relating to the workshop, whether they could actually attend the meeting or not. Eunice García, Alvin Korte, and Norma Benavides were among those who submitted papers, and their work was chosen for inclusion here because it dealt with issues of concern to all Chicanos.

---

[4] Howard Goldstein, *Social Work Practice: A Unitary Approach* (Columbia, S.C.: University of South Carolina Press, 1973), pp. 186-187; and Max Siporin, *Introduction to Social Work Practice* (New York: Macmillan Publishing Co., 1975), pp. 361-362.

[5] Karl Deutsch, "On Communications Models in the Social Sciences," *Public Opinion Quarterly*, 16 (1952), pp. 356-380.

[6] Loeb, op. cit.

[7] Siporin, op. cit.

During these times, when bitterly disappointing decisions are being made in Washington at the expense of the poor, it is more important than ever to regroup in effective ways to make sure that minorities are being served and social workers are being prepared for mental health practice in minority communities. We feel the "State of the Art" Workshop was a cornerstone in that effort.

We also want to thank for their continued support the National Institute of Mental Health, particularly the staff of the Social Work Education Branch and Juan Ramos, Director, Division of Special Mental Health Programs, as well as Marta Sotomayor, Director, Office of Special Populations, Alcohol, Drug Abuse, and Mental Health Administration. We are grateful for the help and encouragement of the administration of Our Lady of the Lake University and the Worden School, especially of Louis Tomaino, Dean. I want to thank those in the workshop's planning committee, especially Armand Sanchez, and each and every one of the participants who worked so diligently and so devotedly to make the workshop not only such a significant professional experience but also a personally meaningful one. The group truly became a community of scholars. Finally, thanks are due the National Association of Social Workers for demonstrating its interest in our efforts in a most significant way — the publication of this book.

Now we, the Chicanos, must follow through in the direction that Dieppa has outlined for us, for we have only just begun! *Podemos seguir adelante; hemos visto que sí se puede* — We can continue forward and onward; we have seen that it can be done!

GUADALUPE GIBSON

*October 1982*

# Perspectives and Frameworks

# CHAPTER 1

# Chicanos and Social Work: An Overview

## Joseph S. Gallegos

*T*he past decade was a period of accomplishment for Chicanos in social work education. As we enter the eighties and consider the current state of the art with respect to Chicanos and social work, we can benefit from looking at past events and actions in order to better plan future directions.

However, in this article, the author has not approached the subject matter as a historian. Rather, this is an account written from the point of view of one involved in the drama that unfolded during the seventies. Historical objectivity is always difficult to achieve, and in this case it does not seem desirable. Indeed, it was through the intense personal involvement of students and academicians that Chicanos made progress in the last decade. The author provides a systematic analysis of key events from which to draw conclusions about the present and on which to base recommendations for future planning. At the same time, he wishes to acknowledge the countless individuals who contributed in a variety of ways to the accomplishments of Chicanos in social work during the seventies. These include, of course, Chicanos who are graduates working in social work and mental health and Chicanos who are the consumers of services, whose needs have always been the reason behind efforts at progress.

Accounts of the past should be linked to some anchor point in history. Culture as an important variable in mental health treatment and intervention is the anchor for this article. It connects three key areas that will be examined here: social work education, the field of mental health, and social work education for Chicanos. It is the thesis of this article that in the late sixties these three systems influenced each other in such a way as to foster the accomplishments of Chicanos that were to occur in the following decade. The interchange between these systems began to fade in the latter half of the seventies, leaving Chicanos hard pressed to maintain their earlier level of accomplishment.

Today Chicanos must confront issues of survival rather than advancement in social work and mental health.

As used in this article, the term "cultural variable" refers to behaviors and attitudes of Chicanos that make them unique, distinguish them from the mainstream of American culture, and are significant in mental health or social work intervention and treatment. It is the recognition and appreciation of culture as a treatment variable by the three systems described that will be examined here. This recognition became a connecting link among the three systems in the late 1960s, when social work education and the mental health field incorporated systems theory and other social perspectives that shifted the blame for emotional problems away from the individual and gave more attention to the role played by the environment and its institutions in the development and perpetuation of private problems. It was this concern that opened these systems up to a reconsideration of culture as an important variable. Such an attitude coincided with the perspective of Chicanos and other minorities, who argued that their communities did not need psychotherapy or labels of pathology as much as they needed jobs and better living conditions. As a result of this agreement of attitude, an eventful increase took place in the number of social work students and faculty who were Chicanos and in the attention given to content related to Chicanos in the social work curriculum. However, recent years have seen an erosion of this agreement in attitude among social work systems, mental health systems, and Chicanos. A more detailed consideration of social work education and its response to the cultural variable as well as an examination of developments in the field of mental health may provide some insight into what we might expect in the future.

## Cultural Pluralism

The notion of culture as advancing or retarding social functioning was very much a part of the founding precepts of social work. In 1915, Kallen coined the term "cultural pluralism" to refer to a condition in society in which groups from various cultures live together in a peaceful and productive coexistence.[1]

Historically, the concept of cultural pluralism, the settlement house movement, and the structuring of professional social work education developed during the same time. The great influx of immigrants into the United States between 1885 and 1920 created stresses on American society and gave impetus to the professionalization of the field of social work. For these new immigrants, predominantly eastern European Jews and groups from southern Europe, the imperative was to assimilate or perish. They suffered indignities of class and ethnic discrimination, and their problems of adaptation and adjustment in this country became the focus of much social work activity.

Concurrent with the conceptual development of cultural pluralism was the social settlement movement. The social settlements, the most famous of which was Chicago's Hull House, first appeared in the slums of major American cities in the 1890s. The experience of those who worked in these projects brought them a new understanding and appreciation of the immigrants and their heritages. As a result, social workers were among the first to question the usual process of assimilation and to call for a recognition of the value of ethnic traditions and the benefits they might bring to American life.[2] Basically, they were concerned about the immigrant forced into an assimilation that almost inevitably diminished self-respect and divided families along generational lines. Assimilation could be made considerably more palatable, they thought, if the immigrant were encouraged to believe that his or her background was something to be proud of rather than something to be cast off as quickly as possible. In addition, settlement workers were convinced that immigrant heritages had positive contributions to make to American culture.

Of all the settlement leaders, by far the most prominent was Jane Addams, founder of Hull House. Rather than ignoring the immigrants' experience and traditions in preparing them for "practical citizenship," she believed that it was necessary "to preserve and keep whatever of value their past life contained."[3] For Addams, as for the others, the benefits to be derived from emphasizing and preserving items of value from immigrant heritages did not accrue to the immigrant alone. The nation as a whole could gain from this variety of experience. She noted, for example, that immigrants frequently brought skills to this country, which might be of great value to American life if they were "intelligently studied and developed."[4] On a less tangible level, she observed that the United States had "fallen into the Anglo-Saxon temptation of governing all peoples by one standard" and implied that the presence of different ethnic groups could lead to a better form of democracy based on "the experiences and hopes of all the varied peoples among us."[5] Moreover, the existence of this diversity might of necessity bring the nation to a greater understanding of those "basic and essential likenesses" of human nature that transcended more external differences."[6] Finally, Addams thought that the experience of living with different groups might teach all Americans a broader, more cosmopolitan form of patriotism and thereby lay the foundations for a new international order. "There arises the hope," she wrote, "that when this newer patriotism becomes large enough, it will overcome arbitrary boundaries and soak up the notion of nationalism."[7]

Thus did Addams and her contemporaries in the social settlement movement question and seek to modify the usual notions of Americanization. Their experience in working with immigrants enabled them to find virtue in the diversity that so greatly troubled many other Americans, and they regarded it as part of their mission to publicize these findings and the conclusions to which they led. Actually, however, their views did not challenge traditional concepts. Their purpose in emphasizing the worth of ethnic heritage was to temper assimilation, not to abandon it. Moreover, the idea that immigrants could contribute "items of value" to the development of national life implied that out of a present American diversity would come a new and enriched American unity. Presumably, the "older Americans" would decide what was of value and, therefore, worth preserving, and what was not. In short, if the social settlement people sought to ease the pains of adjustment, their goal, despite their liberal approach, was ultimately one of assimilation. They did not question the end, but the means, and the end was the absorption of the immigrant into a homogeneous society.

The end of the social reform period, as it has come to be known, was marked by the movement of social work toward the psychoanalytic model. Within this framework, the stress is upon understanding problems in the individual, not in society. As Axinn and Levin state, "therapy had become the door to well being."[8] We can speculate that the decrease in immigration and the increased pressures of patriotism and assimilation caused by World War I, World War II, and the years of the Great Depression contributed to the move away from considerations of cultural pluralism.

From the 1930s to the 1950s there was little concern with issues of pluralism, so entrenched had the intrapsychic approach to human problems become. Occasional confrontations in race relations were seen as indications of this country's failure to assimilate minorities of color because of their own deviant and resistant natures. With the gains in civil rights legislation in the late fifties and with the War on Poverty in the sixties, minorities of color began to see a broadening of life choices and opportunities. Hence, there was a renewed social and political interest in pluralism. These shifts in interest are reflected in the curriculum offerings of schools of social work over the years.

## Curriculum Developments

As social work became professionalized, curriculum content on ethnicity and group identity did not receive much attention. There are a few notable exceptions. Before World War I, the New York School of Philanthropy offered a course entitled "Racial Traits in the Population." After the war, ethnicity played a part in the establishment of the

Training School for Jewish Social Work. Founded in 1925, this school lasted until 1940, when it closed as a result of financial problems.[9] In general, however, from the 1920s to the 1940s social work curricula were dominated by analytically oriented material on human personality.[10] A review of the literature in regard to minority content in social work curricula indicates that prior to 1968 little research or writing focused on minority group people and their plight in the United States.[11]

The impetus for a more formal commitment to recruiting minority group members to social work education, both as faculty and students, and to develop curriculum materials on minorities began in 1968 under the direction of the Council on Social Work Education (CWSE). At this time disenchantment was growing among minority people and others with the psychotherapeutic approach in social work, which emphasized helping the client develop mechanisms or abilities for coping with stress. By focusing on modifying individual behavior rather than on restructuring society or elements of the social system, social work education had been tied both ideologically and conceptually to a monocultural, dominant community. This was no longer acceptable. Demands were made for restructuring the curriculum to reflect the concerns of minorities by including techniques and tools for effecting social and organizational change. Out of this effort grew the Commission on Minority Groups of the CSWE, and the establishment of Accreditation Standard 1234A. This standard required all schools of social work to demonstrate racial, cultural, and social diversity in students, faculty, and curriculum, stating that "A school must make special, continual efforts to enrich its program by providing racial, ethnic, and cultural diversity in its student body and at all levels of instructional and research personnel, and by providing corresponding educational supports."[12] In essence, the standard was based on the recognition that an appreciation of cultural diversity should be a value basic to the profession and to practicing social workers.

With the advent of the new policy represented by standard 1234A, courses proliferated, often with little thought being given to the manner in which minority content would be addressed and to what end it would be initiated. Results were uneven, as can be seen by considering highlights of the curriculum development process in regard to minority content in social work education. These can be reviewed in terms of the following areas: historical facts about minority status, practice methods, commitment to recruitment and demands for social justice for minorities, and the emergence of a new pluralism in social work education.

## Historical Facts

The social ferment of the 1960s catapulted social work education into the area of economic, social, and ideological disparities between minority and nonminority groups. It was found that the hurdles leading to racial equality were high and that extraordinary preparations had to be made for each leap. The most direct mode of offsetting some of the problems encountered was thought to reside in programs of learning. Most students came to schools of social work knowing very little, if anything, about the history of racial minorities in the United States. Increased knowledge, it was argued, would help eliminate stereotypes. One way of augmenting students' knowledge was to make use of numbers of articles and books being written about minority people in America in a historical context. At the MSW level, courses in the history of blacks, Chicanos, and other groups reflected this concern. The historical approach served its function, but once students absorbed the facts about various minority groups, they needed more to make the facts relevant. Facts alone did not lead to appropriate intervention.

## Methods

The how-to courses that ensued were concerned with teaching social work students the rudiments of working in a cross-cultural context, for educators felt the need to make the casework method more effective in developing the identity and uniqueness of minority clients. Such journal articles as "Race and Its Relevance to Transference," "The White Professional and the Black Client," "Black Patient–White Therapist," and "Education for Practice with Minorities" were indicative of the focus at that time.[13] The emphasis was on specific situations, for broad knowledge was not yet developed, much less integrated, throughout the curriculum. Attention to minority content continued to be erratic.

## Recruitment

As the decade of the sixties came to a close, minority group members were underrepresented in schools of social work. Because social workers were rapidly becoming the primary professionals in mental health centers and agencies and relatively few minority group members were numbered among them, affirmative action became a national issue in mental health. Many believed that the lack of minority mental health workers contributed to the underutilization of mental health services by minority groups.

At this time, minorities themselves pressured schools to increase their enrollment of minority students. The concern of these groups was that nonminority practitioners could not empathize with minority problems or provide culture-specific services. However, national needs for minority mental health workers and pressure from minority groups were forces external to the social work profession. Accreditation Standard 1234A provided an internal rationale for the recruitment of minority students.

As stated in the "Guidelines for Implementation" for 1234A, the overriding purpose of the standard was to heighten students' awareness of the United States as a pluralistic society and of the importance of an understanding of cultural diversity for sensitive and effective social work intervention.[14] The guidelines further stated that a basic principle from which the standard was derived was that the resolution of social problems in this society requires an understanding of racial, cultural, and social differences and that this understanding could result from involvement and interaction with different groups in society.

The implication here was that descriptive and experiential content in the social work curriculum would be enough to inculcate in the student the knowledge necessary to operate as a sensitive and effective social worker in a pluralistic society. Accordingly, this approach was implemented mainly through the use of content on the history of minorities, courses in black studies and in issues of concern to Chicanos and other groups, and sensitizing group-encounter courses. It also provided the logic to support an increase in the number of minority students and faculty, for such an increase would enable social work students to have greater opportunities to participate in cross-cultural interaction and to gain in their knowledge of others. But however meritorious it may have been as a first step, the approach taken was inadequate, because it discounted the importance of a substantive theoretical knowledge base for an understanding of cultural, racial, and social differences. In addition, it placed great strain on minority students and faculty to be culture experts and did not provide the additional structural supports needed by minority students and faculty.

Almost a decade later, Scott observed that in spite of the recognized need within minority communities, minority students constituted only 20 percent of the full-time master's students in schools of social work.[15] His data indicated a downward trend after 1973. But also noteworthy was the fact that minority enrollment was not equally distributed across the country. Minorities were represented at schools in areas with heavy concentrations of minorities. Minority-specific programs such as at Howard University, San Jose State University, and the University of Puerto Rico tended to skew the representativeness of the data. Therefore, it is important to recognize that Scott's conclusions are based on aggregate data. Allowances must be made for the fact that totals such as his reflect the operation of schools committed to the recruitment and training of specific minority groups, such as Howard University. Such totals mask the existence of other schools that continue a history of nonminority representation. Each school of social work must, then, be assessed in light of its own record relative to its regional location and the minority composition of the local population.

In summary, minority recruitment has not been a sustained success for social work. Despite the investment of federal resources in financial aid and training programs, and despite the desires of minority individuals and communities, schools have not been able to respond in an effective programmatic manner. They have failed to recognize that although providing financial assistance is important for retention and successful matriculation of minority students, schools also need to provide minority content, minority faculty, and minority support systems.

## The New Pluralism

The most recent phase in social work education has included the concept of pluralism. It is an attempt to operationalize the egalitarian ideals on which the profession was founded as well as to make the delivery of social work services responsive, relevant, and appropriate. It would also appear to provide a method for the understanding of various minority communities as distinctive cultural units within the total American society. Feldstein and Giordano summarize the development as follows:

1. The major thrust in the first half of the decade (the sixties) was to move social work back to greater contact with the poor and disadvantaged, including ethnic minorities, albeit in a traditional rehabilitative role.
2. The second half of the decade was marked by attempts to redefine social work activity itself to become more attuned to social reform, social action, and advocacy. In large part, this was defined in terms of recruiting and serving members of America's ethnic minorities . . . . an emphasis was on combating white racism.
3. The third state, begun at the end of the 60s and carried into the 70s, is marked by attempts to integrate knowledge gained in the past decade, to separate fad from substance, to institutionalize the valuable changes and to tool up for the new pluralism that is emerging.[16]

In short, the development of pluralistic concerns in social work education that was exemplified by such elements as historic content in social work curriculum, technical how-to courses, and recruitment of minority students and faculty has culminated in a "new pluralism." This new form of pluralism is also related to systems theory in social work and social work education and to the consideration of systems process rather than structure. In a summary of ideas presented by Burion and Flynn, Hearn notes that this view proposes that we think of life in process rather than life in structure:

> We should take a holistic approach based on the principle of nonsummativity rather than a reductionist approach to understanding. We should search for isomorphisms in our theory building. We should acknowledge the indeterminativeness of living. We should recognize morphogenesis as well as morphostasis . . . and we should be aware of the stochastic process which sees the events of life as not random but shaped by the events of prior process . . . . Life process is neither determined nor random. Prior life processes shape the probability of future events . . . prior life process shapes the probable range of future patterns of interaction. Stochastic process refers to the flow of human interactions subject to continual change, within a range of probability of future process.[17]

Within this context, the emphasis on the cultural variable in social work implies a conscious effort to break loose from the tendency to see social work practice exclusively in terms of one culture, class, or nation. It is in part an ongoing process of adding new insights regarding the behaviors of people and of testing values, assumptions, knowledge, and skills. It is an expansion of a limited culture-bound view of people and society.[18]

## Mental Health and Culture

In addition to events related to social work education, factors in the field of mental health greatly influenced the accomplishments of Chicanos over the last decade. The revolution in mental health, which took form in the community mental health movement, shifted the field from a focus on individually based pathology, or the mental illness model, toward a holistic perspective of individual and environment (which included culture) compatible with definitions of problem and need relevant to Chicanos.

The Community Mental Health Centers Act, which can be seen as the policy statement of this movement, appeared to be a catalyst for Chicanos and to present them with an array of opportunities. It promised accessibility; Chicanos envisioned services based in *el barrio*.* It promised accountability; Chicanos saw their opportunity for input if not actual control of services. It promised bilingual-bicultural staff

---

*The translation of this and other Spanish words can be found in the glossary at the end of this book.

through affirmative action. Perhaps most attractive of all, it promised culturally specific treatment, and Chicanos envisioned outreach services focusing on *familia*. The promises were not fulfilled to the degree hoped. Community mental health has moved away from advocacy and community input. It has not made an appreciable change in affirmative action patterns. As mental health resources dwindle, support for culturally specific treatment models is being withdrawn.

Approaches to incorporating an understanding of culture into the mental health system have varied. In one study Gaviria and Stern identified funding agencies, social scientists, and Latino activists as the three constituencies active in planning, and hence defining, "culturally relevant" services for Chicanos and other Latinos.[19] According to these authors, federal and state funding agencies consider accessibility of services to be key in fostering culturally relevant services. Although in the original implementation of the Community Mental Health Centers Act the notion of accessibility included community education and consultation, use of paraprofessional staff, and the ensuring of community input, cultural relevance as a goal has been narrowed to geographic concerns and a focus on the physical location of services. Social scientists, on the other hand, determine culturally relevant services to be those that acknowledge the importance of "indigenous healers, [become] aware of culturally defined systems of disease etiology and treatment, and [evaluate] behavior symptomatic of mental illness in a cultural as well as medical psychiatric context."[20] Finally, Latino activists determine the key to cultural relevance to be the hiring of indigenous staff. They perceive professionally trained experts as too far removed from community problems. For this group, intuitive "street knowledge" is of most value in delivering culturally relevant services.

Of these three approaches to providing culturally relevant mental health services, the insights of Latino activists seem the most helpful. Given the retreat from the culturally relevant social change approach by the community mental health movement, funding agencies have not been active. In their turn, social scientists have contributed little to defining culturally relevant services. Their research, however descriptive, has yet to be empirically validated and operationally applied to alternative models. Activists, on the other hand, have given some clues to the concept of services that are culturally relevant. Specifically, indigenous paraprofessionals determined by Gaviria and Stern to be activists identified six factors that they believed contributed to the relevance of their services:

1. Empathic feelings concerning the patients' experience.

2. A sense of geographic continuity resulting from working and living in the community.

3. A feeling that they also had lived through the stresses experienced by patients.

4. A conviction that their past life experiences had trained them well for their work in mental health.

5. Greater flexibility and mobility than traditionally trained personnel in meeting with patients.

6. Ease of verbal communication in terms of style and ability to speak the client's language.[21]

Hence, empathy, flexibility, and facility of communication are classified as specific skills needed for culturally relevant treatment. In their study, Gaviria and Stern note that language and class similarity are important variables in effective therapeutic communication. Such a match is not always possible, however, and cultural awareness and sensitivity must therefore bridge the differences.

The meaning of culturally relevant services lies in a combination of the three perspectives described. That is, such services must reflect the social change commitment of funding agencies, the empirically tested knowledge of the social scientist, and the practicability of the indigenous experience. Unfortunately, funding agencies, social scientists, and activists are often at odds, and the practitioner and client suffer the result.

Finally, a report on the interests of Chicanos in social work and mental health would be remiss in not acknowledging the very important role played by mental health institutions, particularly during the first half of the seventies. Although support for the concerns of Chicanos came from a variety of federal departments as well as localized agencies such as the Western Interstate Commission in Higher Education (WICHE), special mention must be made of the National Institute of Mental Health (NIMH). The establishment of a special population division and minority research branch at NIMH affected the advancement of all minority groups. These arms of NIMH provided funds for training Chicanos in the area of mental health and for training programs and research efforts. The concerns of Chicanos and of minority groups in general remained priorities for these agencies throughout the seventies.

## Social Work and Chicanos

Prior to the sixties, literature about Chicanos was primarily concerned with issues of immigration and labor-industry relations; cultural variables whose recognition would enhance social functioning were not considered. The concept of cultural pluralism developed at the turn of the century was applied to East Coast and northern industrial cities. Chicanos of the Southwest and West Coast were not acknowledged as a social work "problem" until the late twenties, and then primarily in terms of child welfare issues. From the beginning, jurisdictional debates centered on who was eligible for services. Eligibility currently remains an issue and often depends on whether it can be said with certainty that someone is a U.S. citizen rather than a Mexican alien or a state resident rather than a migrant worker.

In the midst of the Great Depression, local governments found it cost beneficial to make certain groups of people ineligible for services. Social workers participated actively in the "repatriation" program of 1930 that sent trainloads of Chicanos who were citizens back to Mexico along with Mexican aliens. It was less expensive "to send them back" than to provide them with social services. Understandably, a generation of Chicanos grew up resentful and suspicious of social work and social workers.[22]

Little notice was taken of Chicanos in the ensuing years. Racial incidents flared up occasionally, but most attention was given to relations between blacks and whites. Chicanos were one of the "other" minority groups acknowledged as sharing second-class status with blacks. It was not until the sixties that Chicanos began to assert their ethnic and cultural identity.

## Inroads Made

The sixties was a decade of movements: the antiwar movement, the civil rights movement, the counterculture movement, the community mental health movement, the black power movement, and what is often called the Chicano movement. Those within social work education for Chicanos owe much to the early activists and risk takers. The activists' contributions merged with intellectuals' contributions to the theory and ideology of the new pluralism to bring in a new stage of development for Chicanos in social work.

Pressures for change came from the *barrios* across the land and were articulated in social work by a small but effective cadre of social workers and social work educators who were Chicanos. CSWE can take pride in the fact that it was among the first of the professional policymaking bodies to heed these pressures.

Federal agencies such as NIMH and the Office of Social and Rehabilitation Services were soon to provide significant support, as did WICHE. As noted by Sanchez, efforts among Chicanos for change in social work education could be grouped into four general types:

1. Initial development projects established to identify, analyze, and make recommendations regarding Chicanos.

2. Combined recruitment and development projects to recruit students and faculty who were Chicanos and develop curriculum content and materials of interest to Chicanos.

3. Advocacy planning and coordination projects to help organize research and development of social services for Chicanos.

4. Alternative training models to support the creation of parallel institutions of social work education for Chicanos, specialized training and service centers, and specific training centers for the development of training curriculum for Chicanos.[23]

In addition, Sanchez cited a number of projects that grew from these efforts, such as the Chicano student project at San Diego State College and CSWE's Chicano Task Force on Social Work Education and Chicano Faculty Development Program. Training and service units such as the East Los Angeles Mental Health Training Center of the University of California at Los Angeles, the La Raza Training Unit of San Diego State University, Centro de La Familia of Fresno State College, Centro del Barrio of Our Lady of the Lake University, and the Chicano Training Center in Houston, Texas, were all in existence by the mid-seventies.

A more current accounting would add such events as the establishment of the National Coalition of Hispanic Mental Health and Human Service Organizations and, additionally, the founding of the Spanish Speaking Mental Health Research Center in Los Angeles, California. Throughout the seventies there were other activities and projects that demonstrated the attention and investment of resources Chicanos were able to marshal for their people and their community.

As a result of these efforts, services specific to Chicanos did develop. A partial list of service agencies includes: Servicio de la Raza in Denver, East Los Angeles Health Task Force in Los Angeles, the Parent-Child Development Center in Houston, La Olotera Counseling Program in Sacramento, Westside Clergy-Mental Health Program in San Antonio, La Frontera in Tucson, and Consejo in Seattle. In addition to the many agencies not listed, there exist a number of community mental health centers directed by Chicanos.

This account of achievements seems to indicate advancement. However, questions remain as to the degree to which significant inroads have been made into Chicanos' core concerns about student recruitment, faculty development, and the inclusion of curriculum content relevant to their interests.

## Minority Recruitment

An analysis of the enrollment of Chicanos in MSW programs over the past ten years shows a gradual increase from 1.7 percent of the total

MSW student population in 1970 to 2.2 percent in 1979.[24] A direct correlation can be seen between enrollment among Chicanos and the availability of federal assistance to students in the early seventies and its decline after 1975, for the number of students who were Chicanos increased by 73 percent between 1970 and 1975 and declined by 2.7 percent between 1975 and 1979. (See Table 1.) In the past ten years over 3,000 Chicanos have been graduated with an MSW degree. In addition, over one-fourth of the 125 minority doctoral participants in CSWE's Minority Doctoral Fellowship Program, in effect since 1975, are Hispanic.[25]

A similar gradual increase occurred in the area of faculty. Faculty who are Chicanos are overrepresented in the ranks of assistant professor and lecturer and underrepresented among tenured faculty.[26] Reliance on "soft money" for faculty positions occupied by Chicanos has led to the same reduction in numbers observable in student enrollment. A recent issue of *La Red* reported that "While recruitment

**Table 1.**

**Enrollment of Chicanos in Graduate Schools of Social Work, 1969-79**

| Academic Year | Total Enrollment | Enrollment of Chicanos | Percentage of Chicanos in Total Enrollment | Percentage of Chicanos Receiving Financial Aid |
|---|---|---|---|---|
| 1969-70 | 12,880 | 228 | 1.7 | N.A.[a] |
| 1970-71 | 13,990 | 285 | 2.0 | N.A. |
| 1971-72 | 15,031 | 363 | 2.4 | N.A. |
| 1972-73 | 16,099 | 363 | 2.2 | N.A. |
| 1973-74 | 16,590 | 363 | 2.2 | 78.7 |
| 1974-75 | 16,676 | 395 | 2.3 | 77.7 |
| 1975-76 | 16,869 | 399 | 2.4 | 75.2 |
| 1976-77 | 17,533 | 515 | 2.4 | 56.9 |
| 1977-78 | 17,672 | 450 | 2.5 | 62.9 |
| 1978-79 | 17,397 | 388 | 2.2 | 68.8 |
| **Total** | 160,737 | 3,749 | | |

SOURCE: *Statistics on Social Work Education* (New York: Council on Social Work Education, published annually, 1970-80).

[a] N.A. = data not available.

efforts carried out by Eastern schools since the affirmation action initiatives of the late 1960s have brought some Chicano representation to the student population, they have not included the recruitment of Chicano faculty, nor led to the development of programs or curricula in Chicano studies."[27] Regional differences notwithstanding, similar concern can be voiced in most parts of the United States.

## Changes in Curriculum

It is in the area of curriculum development that Chicanos have made the most significant advances over the past ten years. If a comprehensive bibliography of social work and mental health literature related to Chicanos were to be compiled now, it would far exceed the fifty-seven-page monograph developed by Navarro in 1971.[28] Similarly, numerous models of content organization have been developed during this time.

The process of developing curriculum content entails four phases: identification of learning objectives, identification of knowledge, organization of content and of teaching approaches, and, finally, evaluation. At the beginning of the seventies, the primary issue was the lack of attention paid to Chicanos in all content areas of the social work curriculum. Material being taught in schools of social work was being presented from a culture-bound, Anglo perspective. The result was inappropriate practice, knowledge, and intervention strategies.

Chicanos who were social work educators set out to overcome this disparity. The general framework of the social work curriculum includes courses in human behavior and the social environment as well as in practice, policy, research, and field training. Within this framework, key contributions to content related to Chicanos have been made by Montiel in an article on the myths in social science research, by Dieppa and Sotomayor and by Ruiz in work on the perspectives of Chicanos on human behavior and the social environment, and by Garcia, Gibson, Maldonado, and Valle and Mendoza in material on social policy and elderly Chicanos.[29] The Texas Migrant Council and faculty of the Texas Consortium who were Chicanos provided an analysis of child welfare issues concerning Chicanos. In addition, the acceptance of the concept of *barrio* professor, a social work instructor indigenous to the community, who did not have formal credentials but was a recognized expert on the community, helped introduce an alternative approach to field education.[30] This list is incomplete, for there were numerous other individuals who contributed to the development of curriculum materials. Organizations such as the School of Social Work at San Jose State University as well as the Chicano Training Center of Houston also provided ongoing contributions to the process of curriculum development.

Chicanos began to identify a knowledge base in the seventies. Key concepts in that base appear to be the importance of the value of *familia* in understanding the culture of Chicanos, the impact of historic and continued oppression and discrimination, and factors that are associated with sociocultural dissonance, such as bicognitive development, bilingualism, and biculturality. The knowledge base addresses those factors that make Chicanos different from the mainstream and attempts to give direction to the development of alternative and appropriate modes of practice and intervention.

Chicanos are currently engaged in the final stages of curriculum development, that is, in the presentation of organizational proposals and methods of evaluation. The real test in regard to the productivity of the past ten years is yet to come. It remains to be seen whether schools of social work incorporate content related to Chicanos into their curricula, to the eventual improvement of services for Chicanos.

## Future Directions

Chicanos have made significant inroads within social work education and mental health systems. They were helped in the last decade by external supports and the ethos of the time. However, little, if anything, would have occurred without the guidance and perseverance of Chicanos themselves. It is they who seized opportunities as they appeared and fought for every gain. The advances may be meager in numbers, for there is so much more to accomplish before true equity is achieved. Nevertheless, they are significant when measured against the almost nonexistent influence of Chicanos prior to these efforts.

A major factor contributing to the accomplishments achieved was an alliance between the interests of Chicanos in social work and mental health and forces in social work education and the field of mental health. This alliance, which continued throughout the seventies, was not unlike a political coalition. Various groups in social work and mental health systems shared certain aspirations and goals with Chicanos. As with other coalitions, the member groups did not necessarily have identical goals and objectives but were for a time able to work together. Chicanos were interested in social change. One way in which social work and mental health systems were able to accommodate this interest was through an emphasis on the cultural variable in the helping process.

An assessment of the current status of Chicanos in social work and mental health indicates the need for the further development of efforts begun in the last decade. The importance of the cultural variable has been established for Chicanos, and research has been done that suggests the role of this variable in intervention strategies. The knowledge base established by this research remains rudimentary, however. Further research must be done to test the validity and utility of proposed hypotheses and expand further our knowledge of appropriate interventions for use with Chicanos.

In regard to social work education, pressures must be maintained to ensure the continued increase of enrollment among students and of appointments and promotions of faculty who are Chicanos. Similar pressure must be brought to bear regarding the inclusion in the curriculum of content related to Chicanos. It must also be acknowledged that students need more than financial aid and that faculty need more than "hard money" appointments. Each of these groups additionally needs a sustaining system. For graduate education to be a culturally relevant experience, students need peers and role models among field instructors and faculty as well as curriculum content related to Chicanos. Faculty also need interaction with peers and colleagues. Workshops and conferences on issues concerning Chicanos can do much to stem the stress of isolation. In other areas, administrators should actively encourage student and faculty involvement in the community activities of Chicanos. Curriculum models for Chicanos need exposure in the field as well as in the classroom. An attitude of flexibility and openness to experimentation is necessary to promote the evaluation of these models. Attending to the needs of students and faculty who are Chicanos and the further development of curriculum and research relevant to Chicanos requires an investment of resources.

Resource allocation is always a matter of setting priorities. This article describes a time when the priorities of Chicanos coincided with those of groups in social work and mental health. Today Chicanos must reevaluate that alliance. Will it continue to be feasible and, more important, fruitful? Although the alliance helped establish the variable of Chicano culture as important, it has not answered the question of "to what end?" The only relevant goal of intervention for Chicanos and their communities must be that of empowerment. One process of empowerment is resource development, and, as this article suggests, Chicanos have been adept at that activity. Future directions will depend on new strategies, possibly new alliances, and, most of all, on the resourcefulness of Chicanos themselves.

Chicanos can no longer rely solely on external supports and the good intentions of liberals to achieve their goals. Just as current social and political developments indicate a return to a pre-civil rights era of conservatism, so, too, must Chicano and Chicana leaders return to the aggressive advocacy and activism that enabled Chicanos to attain the foothold they have today. They must struggle to survive and maintain their gains while working diligently to build on the contributions of their colleagues.

## Notes and References

1. See Barbara M. Soloman, *Ancestors and Immigrants: A Changing New England Tradition* (Cambridge, Mass.: Harvard University Press, 1956), pp. 172-173.

2. See J. Higham, *Strangers in the Land: Patterns of American Nativism, 1860-1925* (New York: Macmillan Publishing Co., 1966); and G. C. White, "Social Settlements and Immigrant Neighbors, 1866-1914," *Social Science Review*, 23 (1959), pp. 56-66.

3. Jane Addams, *Newer Ideals of Peace* (New York: Macmillan, 1911), p. 75; and Addams, *Twenty Years at Hull House* (New York: Macmillan Publishing Co., 1961), p. 169.

4. Addams, *Twenty Years at Hull House*, p. 177

5. Addams, *Newer Ideals of Peace*, pp. 47-48.

6. Addams, *Twenty Years at Hull House*, p. 89.

7. Addams, *Newer Ideals of Peace*, pp. 18-19.

8. J. Axinn and H. Levin, *Social Welfare: A History of the American Response* (New York: Dodd, Mead & Co., 1975), p. 98.

9. See C. S. Levy, *Social Work Education and Practice 1898-1955* (New York: Yeshiva University Press, 1968).

10. D. Feldstein and J. Giordano, "The New Pluralism and Social Work Education." Paper presented at the Annual Program Meeting, Council on Social Work Education, Philadelphia, Pa., March 1976.

11. Joseph Gallegos, "A Reconceptualization of Pluralism for Social Work Education," pp. 89-95. Unpublished Ph.D. thesis, University of Denver, 1978.

12. "Guidelines for Implementation of Accreditation Standard 1234A," Addendum No. 73-200-5 (New York: Council on Social Work Education, February 12, 1973), p. 1. (Mimeographed.)

13. See J. Carter and T. Haizlip, "Race and Its Relevance to Transference," *American Journal of Orthopsychiatry*, 42 (October 1972), pp. 865-871; A. Gitterman and A. Schaeffer, "The White Professional and the Black Client," *Social Casework*, 53 (May 1972), pp. 280-291; C. Saper, T. Brayboy, and B. Waxenberg, "Black Patient–White Therapist," *American Journal of Orthopsychiatry*, 42 (April 1972), pp. 415-423; and John B. Turner, "Education for Practice with Minorities," *Social Work*, 17 (May 1972), pp. 112-118.

14. "Guidelines for Implementation of Accreditation Standard 1234A."

15. Carl Scott, "CSWE Minority Doctoral Fellowship Program," unpublished proposal to the National Institute of Mental Health (New York: Council on Social Work Education, 1977). (Mimeographed.)

16. Feldstein and Giordano, op. cit. pp. 6-7.

17. G. Hearn, "General Systems Perspectives and Social Work Education." Paper presented at the Annual Program Meeting, Council on Social Work Education, Philadelphia, Pa., March 1976, pp. 15-16. (Mimeographed.) See also William A. Burion and John P. Flynn, "The Systems Approach as Philosophy and Framework for Social Work," cited by Hearn, p. 15.

18. D. Sanders, "Educating Social Workers for the Role of Effective Change Agents in

a Multicultural Pluralistic Society," *Journal of Education for Social Work*, 10 (Spring 1974), pp. 86-91.

19. Moises Gaviria and G. Stern, "Problems in Designing and Implementing Culturally Relevant Mental Health Services for Latinos in the U.S.," *Social Science Medicine*, 14B (February 1980), pp. 65-71.

20. Ibid., p. 66.

21. Ibid., p. 68.

22. L. Grebler, J. Moore, and R. Guzman, *The Mexican American People: The Nation's Second Largest Minority* (New York: Free Press, 1970).

23. Rodolfo B. Sanchez, "A Chicano Perspective on Social Work Curriculum Development," in D. J. Curren, ed., *The Chicano Faculty Development Program: A Report* (New York: Council on Social Work Education, 1973).

24. *Statistics on Social Work Education* (New York: Council on Social Work Education, published annually, years 1970-1980). The original data for Table 1 were gathered and supplied by Simon Dominguez, School of Social Work, San Jose State University, San Jose, California.

25. Gwenelle Styles O'Neal and Carl A. Scott, *Supplying a Critical Need: Preparing Ethnic Minority Doctoral Social Work Students for Leadership Roles in Mental Health* (New York: Council on Social Work Education, 1981).

26. See *Statistics on Social Work Education*.

27. "El Movimiento Chicano," *La Red/The Net*, monthly newsletter of the National Chicano Research Network, University of Michigan, Ann Arbor, No. 40, March 1981, p. 7.

28. Eliseo Navarro, *The Chicano Community: A Selected Bibliography for Use in Social Work Education* (New York: Council on Social Work Education, 1971).

29. See Miguel Montiel, "The Social Science Myth of the Mexican American Family," *El Grito*, 4 (Summer 1970), pp. 56-63; Ismael Dieppa and Marta Sotomayor, *Chicano Content in Social Work Curriculum: A Modular Approach* (Boulder, Col.: Western Interstate Commission on Higher Education, 1974); Julie Ruiz, ed., *Chicano Task Force Report* (New York: Council on Social Work Education, 1973); Eunice C. Garcia, "Social Work Practice," pp. 1-40, Guadalupe Gibson, "Human Behavior and Social Environment," pp. 41-171, and David Maldonado, "Policy, Planning, and Administration," pp. 172-216, in Norma Benavides and Federico Souflée, Jr., eds., *A Course Syllabi Compendium* (Houston, Tex.: Chicano Training Center, 1978); and Ray Valle and Lydia Mendoza, *The Elder Latino* (San Diego, Calif.: Campaline Press, 1978).

30. See Ernesto Gomez, "The Barrio Faculty Component in Social Work Education," pp. 99-110, and Mateo Camarillo and Antonio Buono, "The Barrio Professor: El Plan de San Jose," pp. 112-125, in Marta Sotomayor and Phillip D. Ortega y Gasca, eds., *Chicano Content in Social Work Education* (New York: Council on Social Work Education, 1975).

# CHAPTER 2

# Ideology in Social Work: The Perspective of Chicanos

## Tomás Atencio

*M*ental health services, social work education, and community organization and community development have evolved as the most prominent vehicles for advocacy by Chicano and Chicana social workers in behalf of their communities. In these three areas, as in all areas of practice, the following factors emerge as important: (1) values, goals, and purpose, (2) knowledge of behavior, skills, and methods, and (3) the application of this knowledge in practice. Values, goals, and purpose direct the other two, for one's beliefs and purposes guide one's activities and quest for knowledge. These values, goals, and purpose are part of ideology.

However, the study of ideology has not received the attention it warrants in social work. Some critics state that where pragmatism rules, ideology cannot survive.[1] Nevertheless, this article aims to examine the ideological dimensions of social work, with the ultimate purpose of discerning what possible contributions the minority experience might make in this area. The fundamental assumption made in developing the analysis presented is that ideology guides and justifies the actions of social organizations, from nations to social movements to professions.[2] The first question this article addresses is whether social work is dominated by the implied national ideology. The second one is whether an ideological perspective of Chicanos is emerging and, if so, what its relationship is to that of social work. The product of this twofold effort will show the differences and similarities between the outlook of a dominant society's service profession and that of a minority group that has been a recipient of services. From this analysis, the question of the possible contributions to social work of the experience of Chicanos will be at least partially answered.

# Ideology and Analysis

The study of ideology is a concern of sociology as well as other social sciences. This analysis uses methods of sociological inquiry developed specifically for the study of cultural creations such as ideas, art, and literature.[3] The intellectual antecedents of this approach are found in the writings of Marx, who asserted that people's consciousness is developed by the social conditions in which they live and that this consciousness changes as the social conditions change.[4] Thus, ideas that do not flow from the social conditions of those who hold them are phantoms and fantasies. These ideas console the individuals who believe them and justify the actions of those who propagate them. Accordingly, they are not founded on empirical fact but at the same time are used as tools and weapons of special interest groups.[5]

While contributing to a definition of ideology, these propositions and insights may be used as criteria for the analysis of ideology and other cultural creations. If a constellation of ideas is to be considered ideology, it must conform to the following:

1. Its propositions are not founded on objective evidence and are beliefs that are not empirically true.

2. It is used to justify the actions of those who espouse the ideas and to console those who are dominated in the society.

3. It contains symbols that are mirror images of the prevailing social conditions. These symbols are isomorphically related to social conditions and are subject to change as the conditions change.[6] This means that the world of ideas is a symbolic reflection of a culture's social patterns.

This three-factor notion of ideology is applied in this article to the development of social work ideology. Specifically, this analysis will delineate the relationships among socioeconomic conditions, the domain of ideas and values, and social work. It will examine four eras in the history of the United States, reviewing the nature of social work in each era. Data about the experiences, ideas, and values of Chicanos in corresponding periods will also be given.

# First Era: 1800-1850

This period does not include the rise of social work as a profession. However, it had already been over two centuries since the enactment of the first poor laws in England, and the discussion will therefore describe the socioeconomic conditions in America and identify the ideological perspective in relation to the handling of social problems.[7]

At the beginning of the nineteenth century, the United States was a rural society moving rapidly toward industrialization. Although the country was rich in resources, it was concerned about securing its supplies for the future. America needed markets and access to them. Consequently, it expanded its boundaries to the Pacific Ocean in the West; its trade routes encircled the world. In this scenario, the individual played a primary role, for it was individual initiative that realized society's goals. The ideas that justified this individualistic behavior derived from a religious source, the Protestant ethic. In this belief system, individual initiative was rewarded by a successful life on earth and salvation in heaven.[8] The more capable and aggressive therefore tended to succeed in a society that believed unfettered competition was well-suited to the individual's self-interest. The least capable and less prepared suffered the consequences of poverty and disease. Within this context, the business class arose.

America's population increased during this period, not through immigration but through reproduction. Therefore, a remarkable degree of homogeneity in lifestyle, purpose, and values existed.[9] Almost all citizens were Anglo American, with a common goal dominated by Protestant beliefs of individuality, equality, autonomy, and dignity. More important, the individual was seen as part of a cosmic drama of creation, sin, and salvation. This view justified good stewardship of God's creation—natural resources—and the development of the country's frontiers. It motivated the wealthy toward charity for the less fortunate but confirmed for them the belief that the poor were weak and lazy. The Monroe Doctrine and the concept of manifest destiny surfaced during this period to justify America's industrial and territorial expansion. Later in the century, social Darwinism and its religious counterpart would give new life to these doctrines to justify further economic expansion.

Although these beliefs defied empirical validity, they provided a rationale for the actions of the nation and reflected its structural conditions. The social and ideal worlds were mirror images of each other. The drama of creation, sin, and salvation was played out in the social reality in which people developed natural resources for increased production. In the ideal domain the good and righteous, the careful stewards of God's creation, were to be rewarded with salvation. Thus it was in the material world, where the capable and competitive were rewarded with material goods. In the ideal realm the sinner suffered the ravages of hell; in the material world the weak and lazy suffered material deprivation. The fulfillment of this drama affirmed the values of autonomy, freedom, and human dignity, all manifestations of the divine spark in human beings.

During this epoch, charity, or social welfare, was provided to the less fortunate by the more affluent through individual donations to

churches. Those who did this satisfied another condition of the Protestant ethic: duty.[10] By being charitable and virtuous they were brought
closer to God and salvation. In the political domain charities were
administered through counties and townships that were assigned this
responsibility from the state. Although legislation concerning pauper-
ism was enacted at the state level, local governments were ultimately
responsible for their own social problems.

This arrangement was not sufficient, however. Growth of the population and the expansion of industry brought an increase in social
problems. The only legislative precedent were the poor laws first
enacted in England in 1601. These laws had changed little in two and a
half centuries, but they served as a foundation for American social
welfare policy nevertheless. In the meantime, institutions of charities
and corrections grew to house those who had no other resources. These
did little to enhance human dignity, but they were the best America
could do in response to circumstances and ideology that guided and
justified its actions.

Thus, in nineteenth-century America, individual initiative was
responsible for individual success and for general economic growth in
the social world. In the religious domain individual initiative on earth
and the pursuit of a virtuous life led to salvation. On the other hand,
individuals without initiative were responsible for their own poverty
and sin. Yet God was ready to redeem all individual sinners as the social
order was willing to protect all individuals' rights. Thus were the ideological foundations of America and of its social welfare system.

## Second Era: 1850-1929

By the middle of the nineteenth century, the Southwest had been
acquired through the settlement of the Mexican War in 1848. Industrial technology continued to develop, reflecting the advances of modern science in the rise of manufacturing, mining, and railroad construc-
tion. Corporate capitalism and a new business class became entrenched.
Great fortunes were amassed by a few, and many benefited from
increased productivity. This was an affirmation of the earlier belief that
the more productivity, the more there would be for all.

At the same time, industrial development demanded more laborers
than rural America was producing through reproduction. Immigration
from abroad increased the population, breaking down Anglo homogeneity. Immigrants flooded the marginal areas of cities, and those social
problems associated with poverty, disease, and deviance multiplied.
Unions began to grow among the working class, and city government
tried to contend with the increased number of social problems.
Machine politics emerged as the intermediary for the masses of immi-

grants in the cities and as a vehicle for advocacy as well. However, the machine gained control of city political wards, and it consequently also controlled the administration of charities and corrections. Because the life source of political machines is patronage, political bosses were kept in power by people in the wards and precincts who received help from them. Machine politics grew stronger. Philanthropists concerned with social welfare began to view the administration of charities and corrections as corrupt and the poor as victims of political exploitation.[11]

The religious commitment of the growing business class and religious professionals took a new twist consonant with nineteenth-century liberal thought. By the middle of the century, economic growth had given rise to the philanthropist who was motivated by religious goals. At the same time, Protestant denominations oriented their services to slum dwellers. The settlement house and evangelical missions were the primary vehicles for the provision of services, as the philanthropists used them to channel the resources they earmarked for charity. Their objective was twofold: to evangelize the sinner and to educate the poor. The philanthropists had another goal, however. They wanted to realize the tenets of laissez-faire and use the new knowledge of the social sciences to discern the causes of poverty and modernize and make efficient the administration of charities and corrections. The latter meant reforming the political machine by eroding its power. This setting was the cradle of the social work profession and the birthplace of Progressivism. Progressivism embodied the goals of social reform and social justice and the influence of the social sciences. The movement eventually led to the formation of the Progressive party in the early 1900s and had the support of many social workers, and its tenets were incorporated into the Democratic platform of President Franklin Delano Roosevelt.

Social work in its infancy and Progressivism were almost inseparable. The religious philanthropists and their clerks and administrators were social workers' immediate forerunners. The social work profession derived its knowledge from the social and behavioral sciences that aided in the development of casework services and acquired its ideological commitment from the reform impetus that sought changes in the environment.[12] Two strains in social work — direct services and reform, the emphasis on the individual and on the role of the environment — had emerged.

By the 1920s the social work profession was established. Fifteen schools were in existence, with nine linked with universities and six with agencies. By 1939, the schools' formal association had set standards for social work education, and two years of graduate school were required for a master's degree in social work.[13] During this period, as science affected industry, it also influenced the human services. At first the social sciences helped in the area of diagnosis and in streamlining

administration. Then the growth of psychology influenced direct casework immensely, and casework services to individuals grew, primarily
through family service and children's agencies. The reform tradition
gradually yielded its dominant status. But the rise of social work had
already left its mark on social policy. The term "charities and corrections" had changed to "social welfare."

By the end of the 1920s, industrialization had caused many changes.
The predominant society in this country was more urban; immigration
had challenged Anglo American homogeneity; and larger, socially
interdependent units such as corporations and unions had been formed
in the industrial sector. At the institutional level, the new profession of
social work focused on social control and the improvement of social
functioning as two prominent emphases. The enhancement of social
functioning reflected the older notion of bringing the sinner into the
fold, while the function of social control seemed to have been a
response to the growing threat to America's homogeneity. These two
emphases were necessary to maintain order in an increasingly heterogeneous society and to assure growth and progress. It is interesting that
this dimension of social work arose concomitantly with the myth of the
"melting pot," which popularized the idea that all ethnic groups could
be integrated into the existing society.[14] But it is not surprising that
these ideological developments occurred. Social conditions had changed
with the growth of industrialization and the increase of the population
through immigration. Social work was a manifestation of these
developments.

Equally significant as these trends was the survival of the religious
ideas of the previous epoch and their continuation into the twentieth
century. These ideas were related to the socioeconomic conditions and
social patterns of Anglo Americans and were not dislodged by the
religious ideas of successive groups of immigrants. Immigration and
industrialization brought about some changes in social relations but did
not break the ideological hold of the earlier arrivals. Accordingly, one
might conclude that as long as social patterns prevail, so will the values
of those who are socially dominant. Other groups coming onto the
scene must conform if they are to survive. Another possible conclusion
is that those values, although identified as religious, are primarily ideals
in the domain of culture, which reflects prevailing social conditions.

## Third Era: 1930-1960

With the breakdown of the nation's economy in 1929, the business
class lost much of what it had gained during the earlier period of
prosperity. The working class faced unprecedented unemployment, and
industrial machinery ground to a halt. Efforts to restore the economy

to normalcy proceeded under the aegis of the progressive political philosophy that had arisen concurrent with the growth of industry in the previous era under the leadership of philanthropists. Thus, the same forces that had organized to erode the political machine, educate immigrants and the lower classes, rationalize the administration of charities, and diagnose the causes of dysfunction were behind the election of a president who would institutionalize their mentality in the New Deal. Many social workers were among the advocates for New Deal reforms, and their posture was not inconsistent with the social control function of social work. For although New Deal programs were directed at the poor, the motivation behind them was the need to calm and protect the labor force through social insurance and thus supply the needs of industry. In doing so, these programs would stabilize the economy and restore its functioning.

The New Deal programs progressed well, but not without major opposition from conservatives who wanted to adhere to a laissez-faire course. Amid philosophical debates concerning issues of financial relief, poverty, and responsibility, New Deal trends continued until 1938. The war years brought stability to the economy, with America's industrial might paying off in victory against fascism. Out of this emerged the industrial-military complex, which paved the way for multinational cartels.

Following World War II, Western imperialism began to disintegrate. New nations were born, and wars of liberation ignited around the globe. As a result, America's supply of natural resources was in jeopardy. This pushed the communist East and the capitalist West further along on a confrontation course.

Meanwhile, the East and West vied in making scientific advances. Electronics technology and space-related industries shrank the distances of the globe. At the same time, behavioral science brought forth new insights in behavioral modification, psychiatry, and other areas that added to the pool of knowledge in social work.

Social work moved toward professionalization in this era. In 1930 social workers were scattered in private agencies that were for the most part in big cities. Emerging leaders in the field were primarily concerned with standards for services and worked in behalf of such standards through groups such as the Family Service Association of America and through professional schools. In the meantime, many social workers went to work with the growing welfare bureaucracy spawned by the New Deal and later the Social Security Act of 1935. During this time, a movement among line workers to organize in a way similar to trade unionists emerged, influenced heavily by a Marxist orientation, but its impetus was lost over the war years.[15] The drive for professional standards continued. Line workers in welfare agencies were deemed inadequately prepared to carry out their work, and social work education gained momentum. Scholarly work from professional social workers resulted in increased legitimacy for the profession.

By the end of this period, industrial technology had advanced significantly, population growth through immigration had stabilized, and a new American homogeneity had developed through the "melting pot." The United States was still primarily white. In the international scene, it had emerged the leader. The recovery from the Great Depression had resulted in federal responsibility for the poor. Family and children's agencies traditionally under private auspices survived under United Fund or United Way, private voluntary groups that crossed political boundaries and raised money for private agencies.[16] But the Protestant missionary movement had practically vanished.

By 1950 there were 74,240 social workers, with 16 percent of them having completed two years of graduate work for the MSW degree.[17] A smaller percentage had completed some graduate work. The largest number of workers were in public assistance, with only 25 percent having an MSW. After World War II the psychiatric orientation took hold in the profession, and many who formerly worked in the area of public assistance turned to psychiatric social work and family and children's counseling.

During this time, an ideological posture was clouded in the face of greater interest in scientific knowledge and standards of practice. But the social control function persisted as many social workers found employment in public agencies. In the meantime, the values of human dignity, autonomy, and self-determination crystalized in the literature.

In society at large, the values prevailing among Anglo American Protestants persisted even though the direct influence of religion diminished. And according to the model being used in this analysis, the social patterns of that dominant group prevailed.

## Fourth Era: 1960 to the Present

With the exception of the era of territorial expansionism, the period from the civil rights movement to the present has brought the greatest changes to the economic foundations of this country. Several factors contributed to these changes. One is communication. With new developments in technology, advanced communication and transportation systems have minimized distances and made the world a global community. In the realm of politics, Third World countries have emerged to play a prominent role in the world scene, and the United States, the industrial giant, must deal with these evolving nations as peers. One of the primary reasons for this political shift is the important natural resources these countries have and now control. Today the United

States and Europe must face the consequences of the critical depletion of their vital natural resources in the energy crises the world faces. Neither the United States nor European countries control the resources their populations and technology need. The newly developing nations, aware of their previous exploitation, will no longer play a secondary role.

On the domestic front, urbanization brought a new kind of immigrant to the slums—blacks, Latinos, and native-born poor whites. These groups migrated to the cities, but the political machine that helped earlier groups was no longer there for them to turn to when something was needed.[18] New Deal programs were spent or outdated. Racism permeated society at large and was closely related to the economic disparities between the haves and have-nots. Farm workers labored without protection from organized labor as agriculture in the United States became agribusiness. A new generation of whites, many of them descendants of the immigrants of earlier eras, formed a counterculture and protested what they saw as hypocrisy in the way the government handled social and economic problems at home and overseas. To meet the domestic social unrest and the threat to needed resources abroad, the tail ends of the New Deal political coalition responded by altering monetary policies and spending money through the Great Society programs and overseas as well, in Vietnam, without increasing federal revenues.

Because of these infrastructural shifts in resources and technology and the raised consciousness among the poor and oppressed minorities, other patterns of social relationships emerged among the dispossessed. Riots in the cities, agricultural unions organized in the fields, and radical land reform groups were the order of the day. In the domain of ideas, this meant new goals and new values, and the goals of social control and restoration of social functioning were criticized. The concepts of human dignity and autonomy as well as their derivative, self-determination, were seen in a new light, as tools of social control.[19] Dignity came from the ability to change conditions that impaired human fulfillment. Autonomy and self-determination were empty words without the improvement of conditions. At the same time, Great Society programs introduced the policy of maximum feasible participation. For the first time, consumers of social services could participate in policymaking for programs designed to serve them.

Social work, the profession charged with enhancing social functioning and assuring social control while supporting human autonomy and dignity, was caught amid new trends. In response, it reclaimed its heritage from the reform movement, as social workers argued that today's social action was like the reform movement of the past. In reality, it was not. Reform had been part of the Progressive movement that sought to streamline the administration of social welfare, use scientific knowledge to solve human problems, and improve conditions for the poor. In contrast, modern social activists called for structural changes, equitable distribution of income, and justice in the political sphere. During this time, new concepts and terms cropped up in the literature, among them ideological advocacy, legal rights to services, and attack on the medical model. Casework continued to be practiced in individual treatment in various fields, with the most prominent being psychiatry. Some social workers ventured into private practice, while others formed linkages with physicians to carry out their work and receive third-party payments. The number of schools offering doctoral degrees in research increased, as did the number of social workers in medical school facilities. Many, however, still worked in agencies in areas ranging from public assistance to child guidance to Veterans Administration hospitals.

But the most important change came in new fields where the new rhetoric could be realized in action, primarily the fields of community action and development; community organization, which took a new direction toward a more active role in the community and less involvement in coordination and fund raising; mental health services, which were greatly expanded; and consumer advocacy. All these areas mirrored the perceived needs of minorities. However, these trends required social work to adjust. They called for new knowledge and new methods. Thus, the need to develop appropriate curricula was articulated, and social work education came into the spotlight.

These developments threw the isomorphic, or mirror, relationship between dominant social conditions and ideas and values into convulsions. Traditional American values still reflected the dominant society, and social work operated under their guidance. But the new consciousness and new awareness among the poor and minorities began to be manifested in the quest for new values and new goals that were not reflected in the dominant structures. America was experiencing an ideological crisis.

At this time Chicanos came into the picture as they began to make themselves heard. The dominant ideology was questioned by them; a new one began to emerge.[20] A discussion of the experience of Chicanos through the four eras just described will aid in determining the emerging ideology of Chicanos and its implications for social work theory and practice.

## Early Experience

During the period from 1800 to 1850, Mexicans in what is now the southwestern part of the United States experienced dramatic changes in their government. Until 1821 the region had been part of northern New Spain, but that year Mexico made it part of its new nation after gaining independence from Spain. That period of independence lasted less than thirty years before the Southwest became part of the United States. At this juncture, Mexican Americans in California were dislodged from their moorings, lost their vast *haciendas,** were reduced to the lower levels of the occupational hierarchy, and retreated to the *barrio*. Their homes were the Old Towns, or *Pueblos Viejos*, the birthplaces of many southwestern cities.[21] The church ministered to their spiritual needs, but relationships based on reciprocity formed the base for the services Mexicans received from and provided to one another. During this time New Mexico, the oldest part of the Mexican Southwest in terms of the Spanish presence, was practically divested of its major resource, its land, as a result of the presence of the United States. American lawyers changed laws relating to land ownership and gradually came to possess many of the vast land grants Spain and Mexico had given their settlers. As land was lost and stock raising diminished in New Mexico, subsistence agriculture continued. The village structure provided a form of social security as did the *barrios* in the city. Mutual aid and reciprocity were the sources of this support.

Many people were already living under adverse conditions in a subsistence economy within a harsh environment, and the loss of land did not affect them immediately. It is thus no surprise that at the ideal level values relating to harmony with nature, reciprocity, faith in God and destiny, and respect for authority prevailed. People had to share in order to survive, nature provided sustenance, and in periods of natural disasters, faith in God restored hope for a better future. In the real world, the *patrón*, the ruling elder of the village, or the *hacienda* owner must be respected, as were all elders in authority. In the ideal world, God held all the cards determining one's lot in life. These values are found in preindustrial societies and in the mythological-religious roots of Indian culture.

The beliefs tied to them conform to the criteria for ideology outlined earlier. That is, they are not empirically true, they seem to console the individual for an underclass status, and they have some isomorphic relationships with the real world. Because of an ideological blackout prevailing since the American conquest of the Southwest, many of these values and symbols have not been reflected in the literature of Chicanos. Thus oral history and folklore yield much of this material today.

---

*The translation of this and other Spanish words can be found in the glossary at the end of this book.

The period between 1850 and 1929 was basically similar. A pattern of *barrio* settlement with Mexicans at the bottom of the occupational structure had been established since the American conquest. Consequently, as other Mexicans immigrated to the United States, they lived in the *barrios* and filled jobs other Mexicans before them had occupied.[22] Many worked in mines, creating Mexican mining communities; others worked in the fields. But very few Mexican Americans moved up the occupational ladder.

The same social factors salient in the history of social work, such as capitalism and the trade union movement, appeared during this time, but the values of Mexican Americans continued to reflect their preindustrial and underclass condition. They practiced reciprocity in mutual aid societies, *sociedades de mutua protección*, which were basically burial societies that provided social support to their members at all times, and in attempts to form unions in the mining camps. (However, these attempts often led to conflicts in the camps.) The colonial mentality prevailed and mythological-religious ideas predominated.

Although in the 1930s Mexican Americans were at the lower end of the social and economic scale, basically unreached by social services in labor camps, villages, or *barrios*, World War II opened new avenues of geographic and social mobility. Some went into military service; others followed the defense industry and were given jobs within the industrial machine. Following the war, greater educational opportunities became available. These new opportunities broke down Mexican American homogeneity to a degree, but traditional values still prevailed. The *barrios* and villages continued to provide a vehicle for primary social relations.

In New Mexico the erosion of the land base proceeded, and welfare served as a poor substitute to meet the needs of the people. Another type of colonial mentality developed—dependence. Those who escaped it did so by accepting the values of the dominant society, adjusting to its demands, and benefiting, though meagerly, from its resources. Their values changed as they climbed up the ladder, and the person who had a safe middle-class job accepted middle-class values.

## The Sixties and Beyond

However, assimilation and acculturation were not for everybody. Some could not achieve them; others were not willing to pay the price. By the 1960s those in the marginal parts of society—farm workers, *barrio* dwellers who had been victimized by the system, and those whose families had lost their land in New Mexico—surged forward to demand their rights, justice, and their land. This followed the black civil rights movement and coincided with antiwar activities.

In the streets of Los Angeles, Denver, and other cities where Mexican Americans lived, the term "Chicano" unified youths and made older members of the Mexican American community cringe. It signaled for one group political unification around the issue of ethnicity and for the other the possible loss of all they had gained by accommodating to the dominant structures. It became clear that a colonial mentality still existed, with young people because they acted to shed it, with the acculturated group because they were still uneasy about affirming their identity despite previous and current injustices. But the movement to affirm the identity of Chicanos caught on, bringing groups of professionals together with the victims of societal forces. Analyses were made by scholars emerging among Chicanos, and the ideological blackout that had existed since the American conquest was lifted as both social science and creative literature found expression in publications such as *El Grito*. Newspapers associated with the "Chicano movement," as it was called, proliferated and reached a wide audience. In them, traditional Anglo American values were questioned and new goals, purposes, and values advanced.

When the movement began and an analysis of historical conditions was made, one of the first affirmations was of Chicanos' Indian roots. The mythological-religious factor in the domain of ideas was suggested as the wellspring of the traditional values of Chicanos. A most striking manifestation of this assertion was the revival of the myth of Aztlan in the form of a political action plan. According to Mares, the core of this myth is the belief that the homeland of the Aztecs was somewhere in what is today the southwestern part of the United States.[23] The Aztecs left their homeland to wander south and by the fourteenth century settled in the valley of Mexico. Many adherents of the movement to affirm the identity of Chicanos felt they wanted to reclaim this homeland, which the Aztecs called Aztlan, as a rightful part of their heritage. In political terms, this meant that the five southwestern states previously the territory of Mexico and later part of the United States would compose a new nation—the nation of Chicanos. In addition, Indian mythology began to give direction to many activities in other areas, among them the rise of the occult and the use of native spiritual and herbal healers, *curanderos*, in mental health and other human services. Traditional Christian institutions and some principles of Christianity were denigrated. All that was white and European was derided.

The affirmation of myth by Chicanos is a case of ideas being promulgated in an attempt to change the societal infrastructure. However, materialists would view the myth as directly connected to the current economic reality. Oppressed and powerless people create political myths as a means of consolation and justification for their condition, but movements that begin at the level of the political or ideological cannot succeed in changing the sociocultural system.[24] Whatever the reason and whatever the impetus, the myth of Aztlan served a strong ideological purpose. It was the source of new or alternative values and provided another epistemological perspective.

Another conclusion of the movement's analysis was that Chicanos made up an internal colony. This explained the economic exploitation and underclass status endured by most Chicanos since the American conquest. Urbanization and industrialization resulted in the exploitation of those on the periphery of the centers of power, and Chicanos had been on the periphery since the 1848 settlement of the war.[25] Armed with the myth of Aztlan, the movement to affirm their identity was to help change this. However, many took a moderate stance and sought change through increased participation in the system. But for a time all advocates of change sought alternative institutions in every area, including health services. Great Society programs offered support through a policy of consumer participation, and for a while alternative institutions flourished. In a way, the push for content related to Chicanos in traditional social work education and practice is one such alternative. Were integration into the total body of professional knowledge to occur, the thoughts and ideas of Chicanos derived from their own research would gain legitimacy within social work. Then social workers who were Chicanos would receive education and training based on the uniqueness of their own social and cultural experiences.

The new analysis emerging from the movement emphasizing a separate identity showed that the segmented society in which Chicanos were treated as an internal colony went hand in glove with institutional racism. To be Mexican or a Chicano or Chicana coincided with a low position in the occupational hierarchy.[26] This was the case in all institutions, including those in the area of mental health and other social services. Chicanos attempted to change this and made big gains in the occupational arena through affirmative action programs.

## New Perspectives

Chicanos' identification and acceptance of their Indian roots may perhaps have more radical implications for them than any other contribution of the movement to affirm their identity. Were Chicanos to follow the Indian world view, a different epistemological perspective — a new way of viewing reality and knowledge — would have to be adopted. Some Chicanos did take a different course. Indian mystics from Mexico were invited to university campuses and asked to meet with various organizations to introduce these dimensions of the cultural past of Chicanos.[27] Within social work, a small movement began in New Mexico that proposed phenomenological as opposed to positive empirical methods for building a relevant knowledge base.[28] Known as the Academia Educational Model, this method suggests that knowledge of the universe of meaning of Chicanos is as important as knowledge and awareness of objective social conditions. According to this perspective, both kinds of knowledge, when combined, lead to a new awareness, or consciousness, of the forces impinging on individual lives and interfering with individual fulfillment. They also promote the development of skills to respond to and change the world without and attitudes within.

The Academia Educational Model is a variant of *conscientizacao*, an educational method developed by Freire in Brazil that was introduced to the social work literature by social work scholars who were Chicanos and is used widely in Third World nations to teach literacy.[29] Translated into Spanish as *conscientización*, *conscientizacao* stands as a possible tool to be integrated into social work practice. It is founded on the assumption that knowledge transferred to the learner through traditional Western education is alienated from his or her experience, and it uses the learner's historical and cultural experience to create awareness of forces that impair freedom. At the same time, *conscientizacao* builds skills and develops knowledge.[30]

Rather than focusing on literacy, the Academia Educational Model uses oral history, folklore, and art as pathways to knowledge and universes of meaning. These are seen as vehicles to reach the mythological elements in people's lives and thereby derive values, world views, and meaning structures typical of a preindustrial society. At the same time oral history is also used to reveal the skills of everyday life that have provided sustenance. Individuals using this method analyze the derived knowledge and values in relation to the objective social conditions that have affected their lives. The desired result is the development of skills to change conditions without and to handle feelings and the accumulation of a body of knowledge that encompasses objective information about the world and an ideological perspective. Schools of social work at New Mexico Highlands University and Arizona State University have used this model.

The affirmation of the social conditions Chicanos have experienced, the new insights into their past, and alternative methods of research have at best identified possible new directions for some aspects of social work. They have also disclosed an ideology for Chicanos, a consciousness that Chicanos have been oppressed in relation to the dominant society, and have moreover revealed that under these conditions Chicanos have lived by the values of respect; *vergüenza*, or a belief that individual success must not violate communal goals and solidarity; reciprocity; harmony with nature; acceptance of destiny; and sharing. As indicated earlier, these are beliefs that reflect the social conditions of an oppressed people. The dominant values of laissez-faire and pragmatism are incompatible with them. Thus, as Chicanos achieve social and economic status in the dominant society these values are destined to change, and a new ideology will emerge.

## Ideological Prospects

The three questions suggested at the beginning of this article can now be answered. Social work was born out of social conditions in the nineteenth century that were reflected in an ideology of individualism and unfettered competition. In the midst of some opposition by individual groups and scholars, these ideas for the most part continue to influence social work. The strongest affirmation that social work is ideologically inseparable from the dominant American ideology is its performance of a social control function. Social work, therefore, has no ideology of its own.

A review of the experience of Chicanos shows that their traditional ideological perspective is one of consolation for oppressed people. However, through the influence of the movement to affirm the identity of Chicanos, which created an awareness of social conditions and of a long heritage, an ideology emerged that united non-Western, preindustrial values with the goals of justice and economic equality.

Little has been done to organize these new ideas into a systematic ideological posture. Yet the question of how this can contribute to the social work corpus of knowledge can still be asked at this time. In the absence of a social work ideology distinct from the dominant society, a minority perspective firmly lodged in the literature is a contribution. More important, all groups with a preindustrial memory have a heritage of values that postindustrial society needs. In this age of widespread yearning for "roots," traditional social patterns are disintegrating in the face of infrastructural changes. The quest for meaning beyond material conditions results in a new impetus for the occult tradition. Thus, it is not farfetched to speculate that values such as those of respect, *vergüenza*, harmony with nature, and acceptance of destiny, combined with a quest for justice for the oppressed, can develop into an ideological posture leading to a new humanism. The social conditions of a postindustrial society could well require an emphasis on such values. If they do not, social work will lose nothing if it advocates for postindustrial humanism. It stands to gain an ideology.

## Notes and References

1. Zofia T. Butrym, *The Nature of Social Work* (London, England: Macmillan & Co., 1976).

2. Rudolfo Heberle, *Social Movements* (New York: Appleton-Century-Crofts, 1951); and Anthony Oberschall, *Social Conflict and Social Movements* (Englewood Cliffs, N.J.: Prentice-Hall, 1973), pp. 178-184.

3. George H. Huaco, "Ideology and Literature," *New Literary History*, 4 (1972-1973), p. 422.

4. Karl Marx and Friedrich Engels, *On Religion* (New York: Schocken Books, 1977), pp. 74-77.

5. Karl Marx and Friedrich Engels, *The German Ideology* (New York: International Publishers, 1947), p. 39.

6. Huaco, op. cit.

7. James Leiby, *A History of Social Welfare and Social Work* (New York: Columbia University Press, 1978), p. 39.

8. Ibid., pp. 14-19 and 12-22. Weber argues that the values of the Protestant ethic gave rise to capitalism. This is the converse way of viewing the relationship of the ideal and material world. *See* Max Weber, *The Protestant Ethic* and *The Spirit of Capitalism*, Talcott Parsons, trans. (New York: Charles Scribner's Sons, 1958).

9. Ibid.

10. Ibid., pp. 75-76.

11. Ibid., p. 87.

12. Ibid., pp. 90-110.

13. Ibid., p. 341.

14. E. A. Mares, "Myth and Reality,"*El Cuaderno (de Vez en Cuando)*, 3 (Winter 1973), pp. 35-49.

15. Leiby, op. cit., p. 243.

16. Ibid., p. 278.

17. Ibid., p. 282.

18. Norman I. Fainstein and Susan S. Fainstein, *Urban Political Movements* (Englewood Cliffs, N.J.: Prentice-Hall, 1974).

19. Tomás C. Atencio, "The Survival of La Raza Despite Social Services," *Social Casework*, 52 (May 1971), pp. 262-268.

20. Marta Sotomayor, "New Perspective on Human Behavior and the Environment," in Sotomayor and Phillip D. Ortega y Gasca, eds., *Chicano Content in Social Work Education* (New York: Council on Social Work Education, 1975).

21. Albert J. Camarillo, *Chicanos in a Changing Society* (Cambridge, Mass.: Harvard University Press, 1979).

22. Mario Barrera, *Race and Class in the Southwest* (Notre Dame, Ind.: University of Notre Dame Press, 1979).

23. Mares, op. cit., p. 35.

24. Marvin Harris, *Cultural Materialism* (New York: Vintage Press, 1980), pp. 72-73.

25. Barrera, op. cit.

26. Ibid.

27. Andres Segura, "Continuidad de la Tradición Filisofía Nahuatl en las Danzas de Concheros," *El Cuaderno (de Vez en Cuando)*, 3 (Winter 1973), pp. 16-32.

28. Tomás Atencio, "La Academia de la Nueva Raza: El Oro del Barrio," *El Cuaderno (de Vez en Cuando)*, 3 (Winter 1973), pp. 4-11.

29. See Juan Longres, "Social Change Needs of Chicanos: A Radical Perspective," in Sotomayor and Ortega y Gasca, eds. *Chicano Content in Social Work Education*.

30. Paulo Freire, *Pedagogy of the Oppressed* (New York: Herder and Herder, 1968).

# CHAPTER 3

# Evaluating Approaches to Practice

### Ronald C. Bounous

O ver the last twenty years there have been a number of significant efforts to describe and analyze the knowledge and value base of social work practice and to develop frameworks for describing and comparing approaches to direct service practice. The names of Gordon, Thomas, Vinter, Briar and Miller, Fischer, Simon, and Kettner come immediately to mind.[1] During this time, many articles examining the empirical evidence have concluded that the effectiveness of most practice approaches has not been demonstrated. Fortunately, this is changing. The present article will neither summarize nor systematically review these efforts. The literature on comparative frameworks is available, and it is cumulative, not too extensive, and should be examined firsthand.

Two articles, one by Fischer, the other by Kettner, are particularly useful for the examination of comparative frameworks: Fischer's because it is comprehensive, listing seventy-nine areas for comparison, Kettner's for its succinctness in proposing ten elements for use in the analysis of models.[2] However, neither these articles nor others reviewed by this author identify essential criteria by which one can judge or modify social work practice approaches. They also fail to distinguish between these criteria and those that are merely desirable, a distinction that may be important in the development of practice approaches and one that this article will pursue. Basically, it will be argued that certain essential criteria should be used in evaluating or building approaches to practice. These criteria relate to two areas of historical and current concern: the knowledge base and the value base of social work practice. This discussion will focus on the knowledge base.

## Knowledge Base

The essential criteria used to assess the knowledge base of social work concern its power. This approach to knowledge is an instrumentalist one stating that the purpose of knowing and of knowledge is to enable the individual to predict and control the environment. (There are, of course, other functions of knowledge, but the question of power stands out as essential.) This point of view was popularized by the philosopher and political scientist Meehan in the late 1960s and is very useful for attempting to understand and evaluate the knowledge base for practice approaches in the area of human services.[3]

Meehan was interested in theory as a paradigm of concepts and in the terms specifying the relationships between these concepts. If one observes the real world and works inductively, one tries to identify the antecedent conditions and processes that determine, lead to, or "cause" a particular event.[4] Simply put, event or condition A precedes or interacts with event or condition B, which precedes or interacts with C, which leads to the event of interest, or, in Meehan's terms, "the entailment." For us this would be the solutions to problems or the goals of a practice approach. The relationship of A to B is conventionally represented by an arrow. This linear equation is a gross oversimplification of complex interactive effects, but, in principle, if we can "load" the paradigm — that is, give real-world referents to A, B, and C and define the nature of their interrelatedness (shown by the little arrows going from A to B to C) — then we can achieve or create a goal or solution. If we can actually manipulate A, B, and C, then we can control the end product or goal.

In Meehan's paradigm, the idea of "concept" is fundamental. Similarly, a practice approach can be seen as a set of statements or propositions built out of concepts that "tell" us if we want to create such and so, then we must create or modify those conditions and processes that "produce" such and so. Concepts are the building blocks of practice theory. This is where to begin when evaluating practice approaches.

In examining concepts, it is important to recognize that they involve different levels of knowing or understanding. (These levels go back to John Stuart Mill.[5]) As one progresses from simple to higher levels, there is an increase in the power of that knowledge—the power to predict and control, to reach desirable goals, and to avoid the undesirable. Each level includes and builds on the one below it.

## Level 1 – Naming

At the most basic level are concepts that stand for relatively basic portions of the real world, such as a chair, a coat, or a light bulb. Our cultural experiences, including our language system, give us a sufficient number of shared or common situations to enable us to agree on the name and characteristics of these physical objects. Unfortunately, this is not true for many common terms or concepts used in our professional discourse. What is pride? What is the difference between guilt and shame? What is motivation?

In order to understand, use, and evaluate a practice approach, we must first be able to identify its basic concepts. The most basic concept is that which specifies the goals of the approach and the goals with particular client groups. We must be able to describe these basic concepts in the so-called real world and be able to communicate this understanding to our colleagues and our clients. Concepts can also refer to relationships or to processes, that is, phenomena that change in some regular or patterned way. This basic level of knowing is naming: what is the difference between A and B; what are their common and unique characteristics?

Most practice approaches fail to specify their basic concepts adequately. Because we recognize a word and can use it in a sentence or logical proposition, we assume that we have the same "real world" phenomena or experiences associated with it as the next person. This is often not the case, and an awareness of this is particularly important when we discuss goals in our practice approaches or with clients. Frequently, unrecognized misunderstandings occur between workers and clients based on their different life experiences. In addition, there may be further misunderstanding regarding the desirability of a particular goal or solution, even if its "meaning" is understood by both parties. If we do not take the time to slow down, listen, and hear, we will remain stuck at this level of knowing or understanding. We need to translate our thoughts or knowledge in terms that have immediate personal relevance for others. This is especially true in cross-cultural communication.

## Level 2 – Copresence

At the second level is the association in place and time of two concepts and their specified phenomena. That is, when we see A, we usually see B. For example, Satir makes the point that indirect, incongruent, or "poor" communication is associated with low self-esteem in the marital pair.[6] The power derived from this level of knowledge is that when one sees A, one looks for, or expects, B.

This knowledge is more powerful than that of basic concepts. It builds on the first level of knowledge, linking two concepts to form a basic proposition, which is a more potent level of knowing than naming alone. The proposition in the example from Satir can be stated as "Poor communication and low self-esteem will occur together." However, knowledge at this level assumes an understanding of what poor communication and self-esteem are. Also, at this level we do not yet know the nature of the relationship between the two concepts or phenomena associated with each other.

## Level 3 – Covariation

The third level, which builds on and includes the second, can be called concomitant variation, or covariation. Not only do A and B occur together, but when one observes an increase in A, one observes an increase in B. Conversely, when one observes an increase in B, one also notices an increase in A. We still do not know which occurred first, but this is a very powerful level of knowing, because we now know that if we want to increase one of our variables, we structure the necessary conditions and processes to increase the other.

For example, we know that a change in significant person A's expectations for increased performance by person B will often result in an increase in the performance of person B. And, conversely, an increase in performance by significant person B will tend to increase the expectations of person A, although this reverse proposition may not be as common. This particular interaction, like most of those with which we are involved, contains a number of assumptions, one of the most important being that person B has the desire, capability, and opportunity to demonstrate increased performance. We are familiar with this type of phenomenon, usually known as the self-fulfilling prophecy, the Pygmalion effect, or "you tend to get what you expect."

## Level 4 – Sequence

At the fourth level, time is a variable. A occurs before B, and B does not occur before A. A rather mundane example is that one must meet certain eligibility requirements before receiving certain social or medical services. It might be noted that meeting eligibility requirements may be necessary to receive services; however, quite often it is not sufficient. Examples relating to the psychological and social realities of practice are harder to derive because it is often difficult to tell what came first. That is, does lack of communication in a marital or parent-child relationship cause resentment, or does resentment not expressed produce a lack of communication? Or do these occur in some kind of interactive pattern having a cumulative effect?

## Level 5 – Causality

The fifth level of knowledge might be called that of causality. It is not enough to know that B follows A. Does A cause B, or is there some third variable or set of variables as yet undiscovered that caused A to change and then caused B to change or, in fact, would cause B to change even without A? At this level we know the antecedent conditions or processes for a particular event of interest, and we have used some procedure to rule out alternative explanations or confounding explanations of the event of interest or goal.

To summarize, then, the function of knowledge for our profession is to extend our capacity to predict accurately and to control in the sense of create those helping conditions and processes necessary for the realization of desirable goals or solutions to problems. Knowledge is built from concepts and from statements about their relationships, which take the form of propositions. The power of knowledge to produce desired ends begins with the basic terms or concepts in a practice approach and extends through covariance to what has been termed causal propositions. In the classic experimental research design, such knowledge is very potent.

In real life, few practice approaches specify the necessary and sufficient determinants of their desired goals or ends in a way that can be put into effect immediately or easily. We have no need to apologize here, for the nature of our subject matter involves human relationships, not laboratory conditions. The interactive effects involved become exceedingly complex, and we have little control over many of their determining conditions and processes. At the systems levels of individual, relationships, families, and small groups, the most powerful propositional statements — those approaching linear causality — can be made about only the most general or insignificant phenomena.

## Knowledge as a Continuum

Up until now we have looked at what might be called the structure and levels of knowing. We have alluded to the content of what is known by occasional examples. However, power and control are also a function of what one knows. It is more important to know some things than others, and there may be some ways of determining which things or areas of content are most important.

The span of knowledge required by our profession is tremendous. Let us imagine it as a line running from left to right. At the left end of this continuum are the individual determinants of behavior, and at the far right end the macropolitical, cultural, economic, and major technological determinants. Moving from left to right we can identify bodies of knowledge relating to the different levels of complexities of social systems. Immediately to the right of the individual we have knowledge relating to some of the most powerful forces in all our lives, those relating to the so-called "simple" dyadic relationship. Here we find role theories; communication theory; knowledge pertaining to conflict, interpersonal influence, and power; and basic exchange theory. Further to the right we enter the level of small-group psychology and social psychology pertaining to groups. Related to small groups we have all the specialized knowledge, different frameworks, and ideologies about family structure and functioning. Further along the continuum we have large groups, formal organizations, neighborhoods, communities, and larger geopolitical units.

In our different approaches to practice with individuals, significant relationships, families, and small groups, we select knowledge from different points along this continuum. However, there is still an important dimension missing from our conceptual map—that of time. Imagine a vertical time line beginning below, passing through, and extending above our horizontal continuum. Let this represent the past, present, immediate future, and somewhat distant future. The point of intersection can stand for the present. Now we have a grid, or conceptual map, for locating knowledge pertaining to the goals of our practice approaches and the determinant processes and conditions of these goals as well as the problems addressed by our approaches and their determinants. Using our time line, we can also locate the causes of problems in the past developmental experience of the individual or even in the future, in the sense that the individual's expectations, fears, and hopes regarding the future are a major determinant of behavior.

Problems and causes of problems can be related to individual psychological or personality functioning; they can also be located at the relationship, small-group, family, or organizational levels. To illustrate, looking at our conceptual map, we can speculate about the possible causes of worker "burnout" in protective services. We can look at personality determinants, lack of significant supporting relationships with family members or colleagues, the supervisory or work group, organizational variables, lack of job security, and so on. If we move the time line to intersect with any of these systems, we can see past and future determinants. For example, looking at past determinants, we find that workers most subject to burnout often came from families who discouraged the expression of anger and rewarded being responsible for others and isolating oneself instead of seeking support from another when under stress. We could also look at economic recession, agency organization, or a person's hopes about the future as determinants.

What one sees as problems, causes of problems, solutions, and causes of solutions is determined by one's conceptual map. Few disciplines have or need a map as large and as complex as that of social work. A narrow or overspecialized map limits the range of our perception of problems and solutions. If we are equipped with only the knowledge of individual psychology or, for that matter, organizational

behavior, then we are going to see problems and goals and their determinants in terms of individual psychology or organizational variables.

Power is derived from practice approaches that can specify their
concepts in terms of the real world in a manner unambiguous vis-à-vis
the life experiences of client and worker, that are based on causal-level
propositions on how to realize desired goals, and that cognitively map
out a wide range of determinant conditions and processes concerning
these goals. Such approaches present a number of interactive options.

## Options for Intervention

The view that everything is connected to everything else, individual to
group to culture, from past through present to future, which was
fashionably attributed to "systems theory" in the sixties and early seventies and is now attributed to the "ecological perspective," has been
present in social work thinking for at least seven decades. It is essential
that any approach to social work practice recognize and capitalize on a
view of the systemic, ecological, or multideterminant nature of physical
and social reality. It is therefore important to ask to what degree a
particular practice approach is based on the following propositions:

1. *Every effect has multiple causes, and every cause has multiple effects.*
   Assume that we are able to increase the self-esteem of youngsters
   by helping them use particular skills needed by their group in ways
   that gain applause from other group members. As a result they
   may be more assertive in the group, at home, or in the classroom.
   They have more confidence, so they attempt things from which
   they had previously shied away. There may be a number of ways of
   increasing self-esteem, which in turn can have a number of positive
   effects. Perhaps self-esteem is a powerful concept. This leads to the
   second proposition.

2. *Many cause-and-effect relationships are circular, cumulative, and
   transferable in nature.* For example, when people learn to solve a
   particular problem, their capacity for problem solving increases,
   and there is also an increase in self-expectations, self-esteem, and
   the expectations of their significant others. They then recognize
   that other problems can be solved in a like manner, which in turn
   further increases their problem-solving skills. The power of Perlman's Problem-Solving Approach lies in this circular and cumulative effect. The act of problem solving strengthens the ego's capacity to resolve problems and contributes to feelings of personal
   effectiveness.[7] Practice approaches that emphasize the dynamics of
   change and growth are the most powerful. They provide transfer-

able "how tos." This leads to the third proposition of selective and multiple intervention.

3. *An effective practice approach identifies options and provides criteria for multiple and selective intervention.* When we realize there are many ways of reaching our goal, we can pick the one that is most congruent with our professional and social values and with our client's desires, is accessible and manipulable (two criteria pointed out by Thomas), is most cost-effective with the fewest negative consequences, and has the greatest short-term and long-term cumulative effects.[8] In reality, of course, one must seek the best trade-offs among these factors.

These three propositions have a corollary relating to unanticipated consequences: We cannot anticipate all the possible effects, positive and negative, of our interventions. (If they are positive, we often congratulate ourselves and our clients; if they are negative, we ask what can be expected in such a complex world over which we have such little control.) This corollary suggests that a good practitioner should be instructed by a sound practice approach to look for both positive and negative consequences, immediate and over the long run, at a variety of systems levels. If the consequences are negative, we tend to be more active in seeking their specific causes than when they are positive. If they are positive, we assume they are the product of the chosen intervention. Are we less rigorous in seeking explanations for our clients' successes than for their problems? When a young client has been able to go through a job interview without an anxiety attack, are we more likely to settle for "terrific" than to pose the question, "How did you do that for yourself?" We have as much to gain from a careful analysis of our successes as from an analysis of our failures.

Being aware of these propositions and corollary, then, we want to select or develop practice approaches enabling us to intervene in ways that have a positive cumulative effect and a minimum of unanticipated consequences. Approaches of this kind may utilize only one systems level of intervention, for example, individual counseling or psychotherapy, or they may use more than one, such as milieu therapy or group, family, community, or organizational intervention. Because of the circular, cumulative, and unanticipated nature of our interventions, and of life itself, any approach will be more powerful if it contains concepts and propositions relating to the variety of social systems that constitute the real world.

To summarize, there are many important criteria for evaluating practice approaches. Two categories of criteria — those relating to empiricism and to values — were not explored here. Instead, this article focused on identifying some essential characteristics related to knowledge. The most powerful knowledge will be that which presents basic concepts in terms of specific, unambiguous, real-world referents. These concepts will be formulated in propositions or guides for action dealing with a high level of knowledge approaching causality and will be directly connected to goals. Furthermore, these propositions will cover a wide range of social systems or phenomena and will focus on the here and now as well as on future determinants of change and growth. They will serve as criteria and at the same time demand worker judgments related to selective and multiple criteria and short-term and long-term consequences.

## Notes and References

1. See William E. Gordon, "A Critique of the Working Definition," *Social Work*, 7 (October 1962), pp. 3-13; Gordon, "Knowledge and Value: Their Distinction and Relationship in Clarifying Social Work Practice," *Social Work*, 10 (July 1965), pp. 32-39; Edwin J. Thomas, "Selecting Knowledge from Behavioral Science," in *Building Social Work Knowledge: Report of a Conference* (New York: National Association of Social Workers, 1964), pp. 38-47; Thomas, "Types of Contributions Behavioral Science Makes to Social Work," in Thomas, ed., *Behavioral Science for Social Workers* (New York: Free Press, 1967), pp.3-13; Robert D. Vinter, "Problems and Processes in Developing Social Work Practice Principles," in Thomas, ed., *Behavioral Science for Social Workers*, pp. 425-432; Scott Briar and Henry Miller, *Problems and Issues in Social Casework* (New York: Columbia University Press, 1971), pp. 30-185; Joel Fischer, "A Framework for the Analysis and Comparison of Clinical Theories of Induced Change," *Social Service Review*, 45 (December 1971), pp. 440-454; Bernece K. Simon, "Social Casework Theory: An Overview" in Robert W. Roberts and Robert H. Nee, eds., *Theories of Social Casework* (Chicago: University of Chicago Press, 1970), pp. 353-394; and Peter M. Kettner, "A Framework for Comparing Practice Models," *Social Service Review*, 49 (December 1975).

2. See Fischer, op. cit.; and Kettner, op. cit.

3. Eugene Meehan, *Explanation in Social Science: A System Paradigm* (Homewood, Ill.: Dorsey Press, 1968).

4. The reader is referred to the discussion of the concept of "cause" in Thomas D. Cook and Donald T. Campbell, *Quasi-Experimentation* (Chicago: Rand McNally & Co., 1979), pp. 2-36.

5. For a discussion of Mill's ideas, see ibid.

6. Virginia Satir, *Conjoint Family Therapy* (Palo Alto, Calif.: Science and Behavioral Books, 1964), pp. 94-96.

7. Helen Harris Perlman, *Social Casework: A Problem-Solving Process* (Chicago: University of Chicago Press, 1957), pp. 58 and 84.

8. Thomas, "Selecting Knowledge from Behavioral Science."

# *Models for Training and Assessment*

# CHAPTER 4

# Community-Based Services and Training

## Javier Saenz

*T*he Minority Human Service and Training Program is a model of service delivery and training designed and promoted by Hispanic Americans to serve their community in Salt Lake City, Utah. Hispanics constitute the largest ethnic minority in the area. The program provides services to all the underserved groups in the community, which include the chronically mentally ill, the elderly, and the socioeconomically deprived. However, there is no evidence to indicate that the model cannot be modified and generalized for work with other populations in need of training or mental health or social services.

Individuals trained using the model are seen as human service providers, mental health workers, mental health therapists, facilitators, social engineers, and change agents. The range of their services extends from being a friend or consumer advocate to providing individual, conjoint, family, or group counseling. This article will describe the essential features of the model.

The program's importance to the Hispanic population and to minorities at large in the area is that it emphasizes maintaining or developing the individual's best level of functioning within his or her own reality conditions, which in the case of minorities are frequently not the same reality as that experienced by the majority of the middle-class population. This emphasis is particularly valuable to minority clients in Salt Lake City because members of the helping professions trained at the local university stress therapeutic techniques applicable to a middle-class clientele. Outreach efforts and ethnic and socioeconomic considerations receive little more than lip service. Although there is a growing awareness of the need for outreach programs as well as for training programs geared to underserved groups, the prevailing attitude is that "professional services" are those provided in an office, where the consumer must meet the expectations of the service provider in order to receive assistance.

In 1971, at the beginning of the program, there were only two Hispanic mental health professionals in the Salt Lake area. Although some efforts to serve minorities have been made through regular channels of services, these have employed few Hispanics and have not encouraged cultural or ethnic awareness or taken into account individual differences of those served.

## Setting

Salt Lake County has three community mental health centers to serve the needs of its 600,000 residents. The per capita income of residents is $6,664; the unemployment rate is 5.4 percent, which is below the national average. Minorities constitute approximately 10 percent of the population.[1] One of the major factors influencing mental health services and policies in the state is the existence of a large conservative population, the members of the Church of Jesus Christ of Latter-Day Saints, popularly known as the Mormons. Historically, the Mormons have placed a high value on rugged individualism, and this attitude is reflected in the state's conservative stance toward social programs. The Minority Human Service and Training Program has therefore had to function within a nonsupportive environment.

The program is housed in the Adult Day Care Unit of one of the state's mental health centers, the Granite Community Mental Health Center. The unit's services include the Day Treatment Program, the Aftercare Program, and the Outreach Program.

The Day Treatment Program provides services eight hours a day, three days a week, to individuals 18 and older who are functioning well enough in the community not to require hospitalization but who need more than traditional outpatient services. Its services include group counseling, activity therapy, family and individual counseling, conjoint therapy, chemotherapy, and crisis intervention on a twenty-four-hour-a-day basis. The treatment program also provides evening individual and group psychotherapy and marriage counseling and runs therapy groups for single individuals as well as health education and information classes for the community.

The Aftercare Program provides follow-up services to individuals who reside in nursing homes or boarding homes in the community and are identified as "chronic" psychiatric patients. The program provides consultation to nursing home administrators and their staff, runs resocialization and remotivation groups, and conducts medical reevaluations. Services also include a weekly social group for nursing home patients and for isolated individuals in the community who are former state hospital patients and do not benefit from traditional therapy. This aspect of the program caters to the older person and to those who live alone without benefit of social contacts.

Last, the Outreach Program extends services to those community residents who have been unable to utilize services provided by mental health centers as a result of such factors as language barriers, cultural differences, and lack of transportation or information. The program serves a population of all ages with mild to severe personal and social problems. Services range from advocacy to education to therapy to providing expressions of friendliness.

## Training Emphasis

Training in the Minority Human Service and Training Program is based on intensive work with the individual on personal attitudes and behavior and is aimed at the acquisition of knowledge for relevant therapeutic intervention. Trainees must understand community systems and resources as well as the socioemotional needs of clients. This understanding includes an awareness of the ethnocultural and socioeconomic conditions of the population being provided with services.

There is an emphasis in the model on certain characteristics necessary for staff and trainees alike. These characteristics include an awareness of language and culture. A counselor who is bilingual and equally fluent in both Spanish and English represents a very important person to the Hispanic consumer. The counselor who, in addition, is bicultural and familiar and comfortable with both Hispanic and Anglo cultures has the qualifications necessary to work effectively in the program. The position that ethnic minorities can be treated only by members of the same ethnic groups is not taken by the program's staff, but it does seem that this model is often more effective when implemented by counselors or trainees who are bicultural.

Other significant traits seen as desirable for members of the program relate to the image they project to clients. Success with minority clients depends largely on the clients' acceptance of the therapist. It is important, therefore, for those training and serving minorities to convey an image of sensitivity and responsiveness to those they serve.

The willingness to provide outreach services is an equally valuable trait. Outreach is seen as the process by which the therapist meets clients on their own ground, away from the clinical setting. The provision of outreach services often strengthens the trust and relationship between client and provider, and, as a result, clients using such services frequently become less resistant to accepting help. The program's experience in this regard duplicates that of Ruiz, Casas, and Padilla in their study of culturally relevant counseling.[2]

## Objectives of the Program

The educational objective of the program in regard to attitudes is to have trainees and staff take pride in being bilingual-bicultural. The objective for those in the program who are not bilingual-bicultural is to have staff sensitized to the clients they serve and to have trainees' awareness of the differences and similarities between them and others heightened. Staff and trainees who are not bilingual or bicultural are encouraged to participate in ethnic and cultural courses and Spanish-language classes.

The academic or technical goal of the project is that everyone participate to an appropriate extent in all components of the Adult Day Care Unit, whose operations are based on a philosophy of reaching out to, organizing, and educating the community as well as the mental health system to a better understanding of Hispanic cultural values. Participants in the program must also take University of Utah courses through the College of Social and Behavioral Science. Classes are taught at the Day Care Unit. In addition to being chosen for their knowledge and experience, teachers are selected for their ability to relate to those in the program and motivate them to reach their maximum potential in the classes. A total of ninety-five university credits are obtained by those completing the program. They also receive an associate of arts (AA) degree, which can be applied toward their bachelor's degree if they choose to go on to complete that degree (the majority of trainees have chosen to do so). Although most of the classes in the program concentrate on sociology and psychology to meet the requirements of the AA degree, the curriculum remains flexible in order to make changes according to the needs of the program. There are courses in Spanish, anthropology, English, and the history of Chicanos in the Southwest. These courses may vary in levels from beginning classes to more advanced ones and may include remedial classes in reading and writing.

Another objective of the program is that trainees learn through doing. Their practicum therefore provides on-the-job experiences that cover case conceptualization, treatment planning, and interviewing techniques in individual, conjoint, family, and group therapy.

As part of the practicum, trainees participate in two case staffings a week, in which they present cases to the staff as a whole and discuss them openly. They also have an hour a week during which they describe the dynamics of a case they are working with to a psychiatrist who is culturally aware and acts as a consultant for this hour. In addition, trainees are supervised individually, by their peer group, and by staff. This is possible because of the administrative design of the Day Care Unit and the value placed on open communication and information regarding patients. Finally, another learning experience for trainees consists of site visits, during which they visit other minority programs in the Southwest to compare their training with that of other students and to visit Hispanics outside their own state.

## Selection of Trainees

The Minority Human Service and Training Program was established to provide entrance to the human services for Hispanics and others deprived of opportunities and not reached by traditional educational methods. Therefore, the program is designed to include rather than exclude applicants. Individuals who are bilingual-bicultural are encouraged to participate. The Salt Lake Spanish Speaking Health and Mental Health Task Force, a community-based, nonprofit organization established to train minority individuals and funded by the National Institute of Mental Health, recruits, screens, supports, and monitors the trainees in the program.[3]

Sixty percent of those in the program are minority group members; 40 percent do not belong to a minority group. It should be noted that the program tends to attract the more nontraditional student as well as nonminority people who are sympathetic to the struggles of minorities. The program seems to work better for individuals 30 years old and older; very young trainees find it too time consuming and believe it requires too much from them in terms of commitment. Some applicants have needed and received remedial courses in such areas as basic mathematics, reading, writing, and English. Many trainees had been unemployed, had been released from correctional institutions, or had been consumers of mental health services before entering the program.

Typically, the selection procedure for trainees consists of an orientation to the program, followed by an invitation to spend from two to five days as participant observers in the program before making a decision to join. The dropout rate in the program itself has been about 40 percent, and there are many reasons for this. After entering the program, some trainees decide to take university classes only, and they transfer directly to the university. Others drop out because of the demands and expectations of the job. Money is also a factor for many trainees. Trainees have been paid approximately $650 per month by funds from the Comprehensive Employment and Training Act (CETA); this may be sufficient for some people but not enough for others to support themselves and their families. The work week includes approximately twenty hours of classroom work and providing indirect patient care and twenty hours of providing direct services to patients.

Trainees typically go through the program in three different ways. First, they may complete ninety-five university credits and receive an

AA degree from the College of Social and Behavioral Science at the University of Utah. Although they may complete the equivalent of two years of school, the actual time in the program may be longer. Those who complete the full program and receive their AA degree have substantial beginning skills in conducting patients' evaluations, utilizing community resources, and providing individual, conjoint, and group counseling. They are able to provide appropriate services and are also able to make referrals to other services when this is necessary. Alternatively, trainees may receive a one-year certificate granted by the Salt Lake City Board of Education that takes into consideration course work, number of hours of supervision, and experience in the program and that enables them to work in the school system as well as the mental health system. Third, after six months in the program, some students may be advised to enter the university full time rather than continue with classes and applied work. These students do not actually finish the program but may go on to complete a bachelor's degree. Individuals in this last group are usually overwhelmed by working and training simultaneously, or they may have a number of personal and family problems that discourage them from continuing. When necessary, this last group is referred for further counseling.

## Training Approach

The three major components of the training model are the Adult Day Care Unit of Granite Community Mental Health Center, the University of Utah, and the Salt Lake Spanish Speaking Health and Mental Health Task Force. The Adult Day Care Unit is the vehicle for on-the-job learning in direct work with clients. The University of Utah, which provides on-site classes for the first year of training and for part of the second, awards a two-year degree and gives a sufficient "head start" to launch students into further university training. The Salt Lake Spanish Speaking Health and Mental Health Task Force develops, promotes, and maintains training and services for Hispanics in the Salt Lake City area.

Trainees attend classes two times a week. In addition, there are seminars, staff meetings, supervision, special support meetings with other trainees and staff members, and, after a trainee has been in the program at least three months, twenty hours of direct patient care a week.

The classes provided by the University of Utah are regular undergraduate classes that use standard college materials but have a practical focus. Classes taught during the first year minimize the use of pencil-and-paper examinations and stress learning through discussion and group techniques.

Staff coordinators of the Day Care Unit in charge of such areas as outreach, aftercare, and training have developed their own seminars for their fields of practice. An orientation course in mental health and cultural awareness is taught by the unit's director for three consecutive quarters each year. Thus, the academic component cannot easily be separated from the more clinical elements of the training. This approach is essential to working with the nontraditional student, who often needs to develop personal awareness and self-confidence before feeling secure in assisting others with their problems.

In the area of curriculum, the technical core content of the training program draws on works in anthropology, sociology, and psychology as well as from such authors as Padilla, Shapiro, and Yalom.[4] The philosophical and technical orientation of the program is intended to sensitize trainees to their own nature, help them develop attitudes appropriate for providers, and introduce them to social and psychological perspectives. The practicum experience provides them with the opportunity to apply some of their knowledge in direct therapeutic interventions. Overall, the curriculum may vary, but it focuses on Spanish, sociology, psychology, English, health sciences, history, and anthropology.[5]

## Evaluation

Various aspects of the program have undergone three research evaluations. One evaluation praised the group program in the work it was doing with the chronic population and underserved clients.[6] Another assessment reviewed the clinical rationale for the program and the rationale for the operation of the Day Care Unit as a group or extended family system.[7] It emphasized the program's use of multiple therapists and the value of using an administrative process that maintains a high flow of information concerning the current status of each patient.

In 1979, the training program received the National Council of Community Mental Health Centers' award for minority service and training. The President's Commission on Mental Health studied existing programs for Hispanics and considered the program to be an important model. In addition, the program was recommended by the commission's Hispanic Subpanel for duplication in other parts of the country.

In 1980, the Social Action Research Center of San Rafael, California, evaluated the conditions necessary for implementing programs involving innovative uses of paraprofessionals.[8] This evaluation described the program from its conception and highlighted the struggles of developing and maintaining it in Utah, a rather conservative state.

It emphasized the need for efforts like the training program and suggested that the atmosphere of internal support those affiliated with the program provided to each other made it possible for the program to exist within a mental health center, despite being relatively isolated from the rest of the mental health centers in the state. The evaluation also indicated that the network of support outside the state from mental health programs geared toward providing services to Hispanics seemed to be the key to the continuation of the program. Finally, it pointed out the transferability of the program to other parts of the country where it may be considered less alien to the dominant culture.

In addition, Utah's state legislature has just provided funds for the program's trainees for one year, and negotiations are being carried out to incorporate the program into the mental health center's budget for next year and thereafter. CETA funds have been secured to pay for classes from the University of Utah, and the university is planning to make provision for the cost of the classes in its budget for subsequent years. Thus, after struggling to endure within a hostile environment for more than ten years, the Minority Human Service and Training Program has achieved recognition as a legitimate unit for providing efficient services.

## Notes and References

1.  Robert Avenson and Marie Wells, *Report on Conditions Necessary to Implement Programs Involving Innovative Uses of Paraprofessionals* (San Rafael, Calif.: National Education Center for Paraprofessionals in Mental Health, Social Action Research Center, 1980).

2.  Rene A. Ruiz, Manual J. Casas, and Amado M. Padilla, "Culturally Relevant Behavioristic Counseling," Occasional Paper No. 5 (Salt Lake City, Utah: Spanish Speaking Mental Health Research Center, 1977).

3.  Funding is provided by Grant No. ST02 MH13715-05.

4.  Amado M. Padilla, *Transcultural Psychiatry: An Hispanic Perspective*, Monograph No. 4 (Salt Lake City, Utah: Spanish Speaking Mental Health Research Center, 1977); David Shapiro, *Neurotic Styles* (New York: Basic Books, 1975); and Irwin D. Yalom, *The Theory and Practice of Group Psychotherapy* (New York: Basic Books, 1975). A complete bibliography of the core content is available from the author.

5.  A complete listing of the program's curriculum and a copy of the trainees' work schedule is available from the author.

6.  Timothy Butler and Addie Fuhriman, "Patient Perspective on the Curative Process: A Comparison of Day Treatment and Outpatient Psychotherapy Groups," *Small Group Behavior*, 2 (November 1980), pp. 371-388.

7.  Timothy Butler, "A Community Based Comprehensive Group Therapy Program for the Chronic Mentally Ill." Unpublished paper, 1979.

8.  Avenson and Wells, op. cit.

# CHAPTER 5

# Cross-Cultural and Cross-Ethnic Assessment

## Juliette S. Silva

*T*he development of competence in practice related to minority groups is of primary concern to social workers involved in individual, family, and group practice, in the design of curriculum for more effective and accurate assessment and intervention, and in the planning and administration of programs affecting minority communities. However, any system of human relations is dynamic, ever changing, and impermanent, and cultural and ethnic systems are no exception. What we know about cultural and ethnic groups is known only for any given time and place. Assessment is one of the ways we can determine what is going on with people at a certain point in time.

The model described in this article is designed to identify the multiple factors that need to be addressed in working with individuals of different cultural and ethnic groups. Although assessment techniques are in general applicable to all people, this model is uniquely suited to assessment and intervention with minority groups in the United States. For the purposes of this article, the model will be considered specifically for use in work with Chicanos and the Mexican American community.

## Basic Assumptions

Traditional approaches to cross-cultural psychology, social work, anthropology, and research have concentrated on comparisons between the United States and other countries. The cross-cultural model to be described is directed toward understanding cultural and ethnic differences within the United States, especially as they pertain to minority groups. The model focuses on three major factors: human behavior and common human experience, culture, and ethnicity. Within each of these major categories, attention is paid to subconcepts that relate to the variables essential to an accurate assessment of different cultural and ethnic groups.

The idea of this approach is to provide a framework within which steps taken in assessment can be systematically organized into a process that identifies means of effective intervention. Those using the model will have a mechanism for the collection of data relating to culture and ethnicity and for the appraisal and interpretation of the interrelated variables of behavior, culture, and ethnicity. This information is useful in interviewing as well as in direct practice.

An integrative approach is essential to this assessment process. A major thrust is the use of experiential learning exercises in each step, which involve both assessment and the formulation of corresponding goals for intervention. These exercises relate to every area included in the model and are designed to sensitize students and trainees and make them feel what the concepts actually involve. Use of the client's total situation is fostered through a systems approach that takes into account principles of interaction among the individual, the culture, and the ethnic group as these three variables are affected by the larger society and its institutions. In this sense, assessment is extended to view human behavior in a global perspective.

The major assumptions of the model are the following:

1. Diversity is strength.

2. Dualism, or the experience of living in two cultures at the same time, is a pervasive phenomenon shared by all people but is particularly relevant in the assessment of minority clients.

3. The consideration of common human factors, cultural factors, and ethnic factors is essential to an effective and accurate assessment and intervention process.

4. Values are a force that affects behavior.

5. Social reality is viewed through external and internal behavioral expectations and responses.

6. The use of a time frame focused on human growth and development, social change, and ethnic differences is fundamental.

7. The pattern of life-survival choices all people make should be recognized, with special emphasis given to those of minority individuals and groups.

8. Coping is a phenomenon influenced by principles related to human behavior, culture, and ethnicity. It incorporates many variables related to institutions and cultural barriers.

9. Ethnicity is behavior derived from a reference group.

10. The assessment of any given problem should take into account the influence of human experience, culturally learned behaviors, and ethnic traditions in a systemized way.[1]

Basic to these assumptions is the concept of change. Human growth and development are dynamic. Culture is constantly changing, and ethnicity is influenced by social change. Change results from conflict, modernization, technology, urbanization, social problems, industrialization, future shock, adaptation, and the passage of time.

## Common Human Experience

Along with culture and ethnicity, common human experience is one of the key factors emphasized in the model. People are viewed as having a humanity that they share with others but at the same time as being unique unto themselves. It is recognized that individual differences are based on inherited endowment, learned values and culture, developmental histories, specific patterns of problems, and personalized styles of coping. When the worker encounters clients, they are at various points in their lives. Their lifestyle, human needs, and experience as women or men must be considered in any assessment that is undertaken. The worker will need to look at a client's situation in terms of the following variables:

☐ The problem as the client identifies it.

☐ Identifying information, such as that relating to the problem or cultural issues being focused on.

☐ Individual identity, which includes a consideration of who the client is as a person and takes into account such factors as his or her tastes, values, thoughts, and decisions.

☐ Family identity.

☐ Age.

☐ Gender.

☐ Place and role in the family.

☐ Developmental issues.

☐ Physical and mental status.

Thus, the perspective of the model is a holistic one, in which behavior is seen as being caused by multiple factors and by both internal and external forces. In addition to being basic to all people, these factors relate to the social role played by the person and his or her family within the larger society. A knowledge of human behavior is therefore needed to assess the way an individual client experiences life and makes decisions. A particular problem or situation faced could, theoretically, have many causes and could be dealt with by different intervention techniques, each of which must be appraised with specific individuals, families, and groups in mind. It is here that the worker, practitioner, counselor, or teacher selects the theory of choice.

# Culture

People are products of their culture and geographic environments, family group, local setting, regional identity, national identity and experience, and social situation. They are also influenced by the particular ways in which cultural issues such as territoriality, discrimination, institutional oppression, and normative behavior have shaped their lives. The worker therefore needs to examine the following variables during assessment:

☐ Original and current national identity.

☐ Original and current regional identity.

☐ Original and current local identity.

☐ Rural and urban experiences.

☐ Generational identity.

☐ Social class.

☐ Economic status.

☐ Racism and discrimination experienced.

☐ Sexism experienced.

☐ Subsystems, such as the educational and religious systems with which the person is involved.

These factors relate to behaviors people learn as members and participants in larger cultural systems. Values and beliefs people possess as a result of interaction in these systems provide a basis for behavior. Societal institutions play a role in educating people for participation in their society. Thus, education, values, and beliefs are culture bound. Assessment determines where people have been and what experiences they have had that have influenced their behavior, their concepts of expected or "ideal" behavior, and their ideas about idiosyncratic behavior derived from their experiences in their cultural subsystems.

Cultural assessment also addresses the forces of territoriality, inter-group conflict, cultural barriers, geographic politics, and discrimination and the ways in which people experience and respond to them. Of particular consequence is the issue of poverty. Too often poverty has been misinterpreted to explain cultural values when the behaviors associated with it merely represent survival behaviors used in coping, resolving problems, and achieving mastery in a particular situation. Social class has important implications for determining cultural behavior. Class experiences account for value-laden action, and a recognition of this, in combination with an awareness of the principles of human behavior applicable to all persons, should modify assessment decisions. Overall, culture adds a dimension that individualizes the human experience and affects how people learn to live and survive in groups, areas, systems, and society.

# Ethnicity

Ethnicity refers to further cultural distinctiveness. People are members of ethnic groups and therefore have both individual and group-related identity, experiences, and social realities. Their special reference group provides them with traditions, a reference language, and other variables connected with a unique set of behaviors. This is an experience shared with others but interpreted by each individual and therefore does not result in a "class" of people or an ethnic "group" whose members think, act, and believe alike. Furthermore, the group does not remain static. The worker will need to examine many facets of ethnicity when undertaking assessment. These include the following:

☐ Reference group identity, which involves the extent to which the person identifies with his or her ethnic group.

☐ Self-identification, or what the client calls himself or herself.

☐ Group identification, or what the client's group is called.

☐ Given name and name changes.

☐ Intermarriage and its influence on the client's adherence to the traditions of his or her ethnic group.

☐ Traditional behavior, which includes behaviors relating to language and communication; roles, such as those of females, males, children, and other family members; family systems; rituals, ceremonies, and customs; informal systems; folk medicine and similar systems; and symbols of identity, such as clothes that identify the individual as a member of a particular group. Such behaviors are measured on a 10-point scale ranging from traditional (1) to modern (10).

☐ Values, which include the client's cultural, political, and spiritual values and the values that have historically belonged to his or her ethnic group.

## Forces Affecting Identity

Identity is not static. The interplay among human behavior, culture, and ethnicity and the integration of these components constitute a process that is constant and continuous in people and defines their identity. Through the distinction represented by the terms "subculture" and "subgroup," the concept of "culture" has been used at times to refer to both the broader phenomenon of culture and to ethnicity based on membership in an individual reference group. In the present model and perspective, culture and ethnicity are treated as equal determinants of behavior, along with the common elements of being human. In this approach, ethnicity and its part in assessment are defined by certain issues and variables. These have been referred to throughout this discussion and are expanded into the following underlying concepts in the assessment model:

1. An ethnic group serves as a reference group for its members.

2. The relationship of the ethnic reference group to the larger society, social structure, and general culture of the dominant group must be considered.

3. Characteristics, values, and traditions of the ethnic reference group and its individual members are important, as are the influence of these factors in the individual's life and how they are perceived, weighted, and valued.

4. The impact of historical events, cultural experiences and realities, and political encounters and decisions should not be overlooked. This may involve a consideration of individual and group definitions of race relations and intergroup conflicts, minority status and its effects, and degree of alienation experienced by the individual. Degree of stress and pressure felt as a result of discrimination, racism, poverty, and other barriers should also be taken into account.

5. The individual's interpretation of experiences related to his or her ethnicity should be explored. Included in this analysis would be individual interpretations of ethnic characteristics, of the experience of confronting norms relating to race and color, and of the particular group's historical experience and the way it has touched the individual and his or her family.

6. The meaning of coping, survival patterns, and decisions of the individual and her or his ethnic reference group should be reviewed.

7. The orientation of the individual, family, and group to problem solving and intercultural or interethnic conflict may affect many aspects of personality.

8. The individual's degree of acculturation and assimilation and success at resolving questions of ethnic identity and dualism are fundamental.

9. The consequences of ethnic status may be complex. Conquest, colonization, enslavement, importation, and annexation may have had profound and far-reaching impact on individual and group identity. This question may touch on a variety of cultural considerations, such as orientation to homeland, and on a range of political decisions affecting ethnic groups, such as the enforcement of policies and laws and forms of segregation.

Ethnicity represents an awareness, a sense of in-group identity, whether this identity is valued or accepted or not. It provides the individual with continuity with his or her past and with a sense of belonging to a people, a history, and a specific culture. This consciousness can also be a bond, an image, or a symbol related to ethnic values, depending on the significance it carries for the person.

Finally, it should be noted that the cultural and ethnic experience of minorities involves the major elements of dualism and survival behaviors as well as the element of identity. Identity, as has been seen, is both cultural and ethnic and is learned, dynamic, and changing. Dualism is related to the ethnic reference group a person belongs to or identifies with and the social reality of the larger, dominant society in which he or she must interact. Dealing with the simultaneous attraction to group and larger society means that the individual needs to develop coping skills as well as a sense of being someone who interacts with two worlds. Survival behaviors reflect the individual's differentiation between the behaviors needed for survival as a human being, as a member of a culture, and as an ethnic person. All people develop an individualized style for accomplishing survival and make choices related to coping skills. These survival behaviors are often confused with the "values" of the culture thought to be imposed on the person.

## Final Considerations

Theory, ideology, and experience are key concepts in the formulation of assessment and practice decisions. Theory is the foundation for determining causation and subsequent intervention. This model uses a systems approach to theory that presupposes multiple causation and evaluates both internal and external forces that affect people. As practitioners utilize theory, they should note the different possibilities for application and misapplication of certain theories to cultural and ethnic groups. They may draw erroneous conclusions as a result of the limitations of theory and of a narrow perspective of ethnicity.

Ideology encompasses belief systems of both clients and practitioners. People in different cultures and ethnic groups have different views of the world, varied political and religious stances, and vastly complex combinations of values not only within the group but within the family. Similarly, for professionals, ideology constitutes a set of behaviors and principles stemming from their own social thought, political system, and theoretical orientation.

Finally, experience is the sum of the individual's interrelatedness with the society and with the world as well. The economic, social, or political encounters and decisions taking place on an international scale affect United States citizens as a nation, as members of minority groups, ethnic groups, and families, and as individuals. All systems react and are linked by the effects.

Given the number and complexity of issues and forces that impinge on the individual, the questions involved in assessment cannot be addressed by stereotypical, monolithic assumptions and approaches. Assessment as a process is useful if it is unbiased and takes into account cultural and ethnic information. If biased, it can lead to labeling that stigmatizes both individuals and groups. Adopting a cross-cultural, cross-ethnic approach to assessment enriches practice and is an ethical response to all clients. It can empower practitioners and their agencies with new knowledge, with a conscious development of skills, and with self-aware, directed action and intervention.

## Notes and References

1. Elaborations of these assumptions, along with detailed information about the concepts and implementation of this model, are available from the author.

# *Models for Service Delivery and Practice*

# CHAPTER 6

# Our Kingdom Stands on Brittle Glass

### Federico Souflée, Jr.

*T*he problem of developing models for social work practice with Chicanos might best be expressed by the question: "How can we develop effective social work practice models for Chicanos in the absence of effective social work practice models?" A less provocative way of phrasing the question might be: "Can we identify effective social work practice models and adapt them for effective social work practice with Chicanos?" This article does not contain the answers, but it will explore the obstacles we face and draw tentative conclusions about where we must go.

To begin, this discussion will reflect a definite bias about the limitations of social work practice. It is that social work is incapable of effecting social change. Social work will not eradicate poverty, discrimination, sexism, racism, or any of the other pernicious "isms" in our society. In spite of our own personal commitment to social reform, as a profession we are powerless to change the social conditions that bring our clients to us. Meyer puts it succinctly in a recent statement:

> Social work can have only a marginal effect upon these [terrible social] conditions, although it has demonstrated some ability to design and carry out ameliorative services to ease their impact. It would seem that the root causes of the economic and social situation in America today, much like fifty years ago, cannot be altered by professional social work methods, skills, or techniques.[1]

This is not to say that we should not espouse social, economic, or political ideologies or that we should replace our terminal values—that is, our values concerning desirable end-states of personal and social existence—with our instrumental ones relating to desirable modes of conduct.[2] It is to say, however, that we should not confuse our social philosophy with our professional practice. Let us do what we have been trained to do best: provide direct services to clients in an effort to alleviate their suffering and their pain, maintain or restore their dignity, and help them cope with their problems of daily living, using whatever methods and techniques are at our disposal and applying whatever models that work with our particular client population. In view of this bias and for the purpose of this article, then, social work practice is defined as the purposeful engagement between worker and client in the joint resolution of problems according to mutually determined intervention processes and outcome goals.

## State of Social Work Practice

In theory, members of a profession are socialized into the profession and acquire a common view and sense of the profession's values, ethics, knowledge, skills, and commitments. Therefore, there is general consensus about what constitutes professional practice and general agreement about standards against which professional practice can be measured. In the social work profession, however, no such consensus seems to exist, and this has been and will undoubtedly continue to be the subject of considerable debate. Intermittently, the profession makes formal, rational attempts to define itself in terms of its mission, objectives, sanction, knowledge, values and skills, or technology. In fact, over the past fifty years, six professionally sponsored and organized efforts to define social work practice have been made. The first four included the Milford Conference of 1929, the Hollis-Taylor Report of 1951, the Working Definition of Social Work Practice of 1958, and the Curriculum Study of 1959 of the Council on Social Work Education. Of more recent vintage are the special issues on conceptual frameworks published as the September 1977 and January 1981 issues of *Social Work*.[3] In addition to these six more-or-less collective efforts to define ourselves professionally, there are in the literature scores of individual perspectives on the nature of social work practice, ranging from the traditional to the radical.

Nevertheless, among the six formal efforts were some identifiable common threads with respect to themes, issues, and concerns. However, there is also, at least to this reader, a sequentially declining sense of clarity of purpose and certainty of technology. Whereas the 1929 report of the Milford Conference contains unequivocal statements about the purpose, functions, and methods of "generic social case work," the conceptual frameworks issues, especially the first, revealed the disagreement that exists with respect to values (social change versus social control), mission (what do social workers do?), and functions and methods (the generalist versus specialist question). Although some see social work as a dissenting profession, others regard it as an acquiescing one.[4]

This disagreement is central to a discussion of the state of the art of social work practice with Chicanos in at least two ways. First, as members of a profession, we cannot help but be affected by the dilemmas facing that profession. To be sure, there are some of us who are clear about our professional mission and purpose and secure about the appropriateness and effectiveness of our technology. On the other hand, there are those of us who, in the face of a constantly shifting, stochastic, and turbulent environment, are groping for clarity of mission and purpose and are concerned about the uncertainty and indeterminateness of our social work technology. However, even if all social workers who are Chicanos shared the same conception of mission and purpose, we would still be affected by a second issue, that of the nature of social work technology. Is it true that social work technology is "soft," "indeterminant," "intensive," and "highly operator-dependent and difficult to standardize"?[5] Indeed, if one were to agree with Simon that "It appears as though it is impossible to address current social work practice because there is no systematic information on what practice looks like or what its components are," then the task before us as social work practitioners and theoreticians who are Chicanos is enormous.[6] For if we are, as Gilbert and Specht assert, practicing an "incomplete profession," one whose technology, developed for the most part by majority practitioners for majority clients, can be assailed because of its empirically untestable effectiveness, how can we take this technology, bilingualize and biculturalize it, and expect it to be any more effective with Chicanos than it is with Anglos?[7]

After a decade of specially identified and funded programs that articulated Chicano social work and mental health practice, have Chicanos accomplished in ten years what the profession has failed to accomplish in fifty, since the Milford Conference? Do we, at this point in our development, have viable, effective, empirically tested, bilingual and bicultural social work practice models based on an internally consistent body of verified hypotheses — that is, on a theory? The answer is no. But let us not be disappointed by the realization that we are only beginning to develop descriptive models reflecting a skeleton of theory about social work practice with Chicanos. This in itself represents a major accomplishment and one to which we can point with pride. Let us not be surprised, though, if we are faulted for having failed to create miracles. Dieppa expressed this paradox very well when, in discussing social work education, he stated that

> deans and their faculties ask us to apply rigid, unacceptable, and untenable standards to the selection of ethnic theoretical and practice content for social work curriculum. They demand "substantive theoretical knowledge based on sound research findings." If this criterion were applied universally to the field of social work, we might have to consider

closing all graduate and undergraduate social work programs, since the theoretical knowledge upon which most social work teaching today is based relies more upon practice wisdom than upon the hard scrutiny of scientific research.[8]

# Types of Models

Whatever models we do develop will be multidimensional, eclectic ones. Findings from the Bicultural Treatment Framework Research Project, with which the author's agency is involved, suggest that an eclectic model of practice best suits at least one agency's small but diverse çonsumer population of Chicanos. The project was funded by the Social Work Education Branch of the National Institute of Mental Health's Manpower Training Division. The eclectic model used focuses on environmental manipulation through advocacy and the mobilization of resources and on individual change. It relies heavily on the development of a trusting and caring relationship initiated and nurtured through *plática*,* *cortesía*, and *respeto* and followed through on with tangible services. As is true at La Frontera Mental Health Center in Tucson, Arizona, our clients ask for and receive *consejos* and *dirección*.[9] The worker-client relationship is regarded as the *sine qua non* of treatment; it is both prerequisite to and part of treatment. It is based on a shared cultural world view and mode of communication. This model incorporates a recognition of the insidious psychological, social, economic, and political consequences of racist and oppressive social systems. It recognizes self-determination and personal choice without fostering or condoning self-destructive behavior or behavior that is harmful to others. It does not impose a cultural ideology on clients. That is, it is based on the belief that Chicanos are at various points along a continuum of biculturalism and that workers need to assess at what point they are and structure treatment approaches accordingly.

In some respects, the eclectic model approximates the ecosystems approach suggested by Meyer. Her approach incorporates theories of ecology and social systems and

> allows social workers to look at psychosocial phenomena, account for complex variables, assess the dynamic interplay of these variables, draw conceptual boundaries around the unit of attention or the case, and then generate ideas for interventions. At this point methodology enters in, for in any particular case — meaning a particular individual, family, group, institutional unit, or geographical area — any number of interventions might be needed.[10]

---

*The translation of this and other Spanish words can be found in the glossary at the end of this book.

This approach allows for the adaptation of technology to the situation instead of trying to fit the situation to a preselected technology. It also requires a broader armamentarium of knowledge and skills than is required of most unidimensional practice models. According to Morales, the ecosystems perspective can provide understanding of the "psychosocial problems experienced by Third-World People, [the] crippling effects of institutional racism, and [the] oppressive neocolonial environments in which Third-World people struggle to survive."[11]

An eclectic model is by definition multidimensional in the sense that it incorporates at various times and under various circumstances knowledge and methods based on a number of theoretical formulations or orientations. For example, an eclectic model might be guided by a systems perspective regarding the human organism and at the same time incorporate an existential perspective that emphasizes personal choice and authenticity, which refers to the assumption of responsibility for one's own existence.[12] Moreover, this model might also recognize the influence of culture on behavior and the perspective that culture conflict is inherent in biculturalism.[13] It would not necessarily discount the importance of the unconscious in the psychopathology of everyday life.[14] What a particular practitioner operating on the basis of these theoretical orientations might do when faced with a particular client in a particular situation would probably be determined by that practitioner's personality and level of professional assessment skills and professional judgment as well as by the situation at hand. Eclectic models, therefore, can be described as contingency models of practice.

Thus, to adopt an eclectic model for use in practice is to accept the existence of certain truths in a number of theoretical perspectives and to recognize the complementarity of these "truths" about the human condition. To do this, one must adopt an open-logic, multidimensional, and organic approach to practice.

The exact nature or effectiveness of eclectic models is not yet known. There seem to be as many models as there are workers, but in general it is difficult to see how any unidimensional model could work in settings with clients who are Chicanos, especially if the model was developed outside of the Chicano experience.

## Issue of Effectiveness

Practice depends so much on the practitioner and is therefore so individualized that standardization is difficult, if not impossible, to achieve. From the standpoint of program evaluation, this creates certain problems in the assessment of a particular technology. The ongoing battle between Fischer and the proponents of the casework method illustrates the research problems inherent in assessing a technology such as casework as opposed to assessing the technicians, or caseworkers.[15] Whereas Fischer's review of the research literature leads him to conclude that casework is ineffective, Wood, in her "study of studies," concludes that it is not casework but incompetent caseworkers that cause ineffective practice.[16] What both fail to realize is that the technology and the technician are inseparable. Whether we call it social casework, problem-solving process, psychotherapy, or anything else, social work practice is the individualized application of a theory or set of theories to a given situation. The resulting heterogeneity of practice has led some researchers to conclude that "the only meaningful question for psychotherapy-outcome research [is]: 'What treatment, by *whom*, is most effective with *this* individual with *that* specific problem under *which* set of circumstances?' "[17] One does not have to accept the assertion that this is the only meaningful research question to appreciate the complexity of the problem of conducting research on effectiveness.

The problem, moreover, is confounded further if one interjects the premise that social work practice is both rational and irrational. That is, no matter how rational or logical a theory may be, its application will involve the irrational forces inherent in the worker-client relationship as well as the irrational forces operating within the human service organization of which the worker is a member.[18] These irrational forces will influence treatment outcomes, and their consideration should be part of any research evaluation design.

There is yet another dimension to the Fischer and Wood indictments of casework and caseworkers: it is entirely possible that both were reviewing poor research studies. The findings of both Fischer and Wood are based on secondary data, not direct inquiry. This indicates the need for us to be extremely rigorous in our research efforts while being extremely realistic when we write our objectives and develop our measurement criteria. A faulty research design can set the stage for failure.

## Value Dilemmas

Given the nature of social work and our country's social conditions, social workers will never be free of value dilemmas. An imperfect world characterized by human suffering will assure this. As Freud remarked years ago,

> We are threatened with suffering from three directions: from our own body, which is doomed to decay and dissolution and which cannot even do without pain and anxiety as warning signals; from the external world, which may rage against us with overwhelming and merciless forces of destruction; and finally from our relations to other men. The suffering which comes from this last source is perhaps more painful to us than any other.[19]

Any model selected by a practitioner will reflect the values, both instrumental and terminal, to which the practitioner is committed. If we believe in the dignity of the human being, in freedom of choice and self-determination, in cultural pluralism, in liberation, equity, and justice, and in the birth-given right to certain basic entitlements, these values will be reflected in the modalities we choose and in our application of them.

To espouse a rigid, doctrinaire, and despotic value base is diametrically opposed to our professional calling. Unfortunately, we live in a society that may be becoming axiologically more rigid, doctrinaire, and despotic, as exemplified by the mind set and pronouncements of the "moral majority." Value dilemmas we have faced in the past may pale in comparison to the dilemmas we may face in the future.

## State of the Art

Writing about the structure of scientific revolutions, Kuhn observed that "the pre-paradigm period [in the development of a science] is regularly marked by frequent and deep debates over legitimate methods, problems and standards of solution, though these serve rather to define schools than to produce agreement."[20] And so it is with us. One cannot talk about the state of the art of Chicano social work practice without first examining the state of the art of social work practice. If Kuhn's observation is an accurate description of the development of a science —and social work claims to be both a science and an art — then the profession must be at its preparadigm period. We certainly have evidence of "frequent and deep debates over legitimate methods, problems and standards of solution," and, apparently, no agreement. We do not seem to have well-defined schools of thought any longer, although at one time we did. Few of us remember the furor of the forties centered around the functional (Rankian) versus the diagnostic (Freudian) schools of thought. Those were the good old days. Today we seem to have about as many schools of thought as there are schools of social work, with few of them being well defined. The question is whether we as Chicanos can avoid the internecine battles facing our majority colleagues, resolve the issues with our own paradigms, and make a contribution both to our profession and to our people.

## Notes and References

1.  Carol H. Meyer, "Social Work Purpose: Status by Choice or Coercion?" *Social Work*, 26 (January 1981), p. 69.

2.  See Milton Rokeach, *Beliefs, Attitudes and Values* (San Francisco: Jossey-Bass, 1976), pp. 235-261.

3.  See Scott Briar, "In Summary," pp. 415, 416, and 444, and Donald Brieland, "Historical Overview," pp. 341-346, *Social Work*, 22 (September 1977); "Special Issue on Conceptual Frameworks," *Social Work* (entire issue), 22 (September 1977); and "Special Issue on Conceptual Frameworks," *Social Work* (entire issue), 26 (January 1981).

4.  See Shirley Cooper, "Social Work: A Dissenting Profession," pp. 360-367, and Federico Souflée, Jr., "Social Work: The Acquiescing Profession," pp. 419-421, *Social Work*, 22 (September 1977).

5.  See Edward Newman and Jerry Turem, "The Crisis of Accountability," in S. Slavin, ed., *Social Administration* (New York: Haworth Press, 1978), p. 310; Yeheskel Hasenfeld and Richard A. English, "Evaluating Organizational Performance," in Hasenfeld and English, eds., *Human Service Organizations* (Ann Arbor: University of Michigan Press, 1978); James D. Thompson, *Organizations in Action* (New York: McGraw-Hill Book Co., 1967); and Peter H. Rossi, "Some Issues in the Evaluation of Human Services Delivery," in Rosemary C. Sarri and Yeheskel Hasenfeld, eds., *The Management of Human Services* (New York: Columbia University Press, 1978), p. 260.

6.  Bernece K. Simon, "Diversity and Unity in the Social Work Profession," *Social Work*, 22 (September 1977), p. 396.

7.  Neil Gilbert and Harry Specht, "The Incomplete Profession," *Social Work*, 19 (November 1974), pp. 665-674.

8.  Ismael Dieppa, "Incorporating Ethnic Content in the Social Work Curriculum," in D.J. Curren, ed., *The Chicano Faculty Development Program: A Report* (New York: Council on Social Work Education, 1973), p. 81.

9.  Nelba Chavez, "Mexican Americans' Expectations of Treatment, Role of Self and of Therapists: Effects on Utilization of Mental Health Services," in Patricia Preciado Martin, ed., *La Frontera Perspective* (Tucson, Ariz.: La Frontera, Inc., 1979), pp. 11-33.

10. Carol H. Meyer, "What Directions for Direct Practice?" *Social Work*, 24 (July 1979), p. 271.

11. Armando Morales, "Social Work with Third-World People," *Social Work*, 26 (January 1981), p. 47.

12. For a discussion of systems theory, see James G. Miller, "The Nature of Living Systems," in F. Baker, ed., *Organizational Systems: General Systems Approaches to Complex Organizations* (Homewood, Ill.: Richard D. Irwin, 1973), pp. 29-63; Alfred Kuhn, *The Logic of Social Systems* (San Francisco: Jossey-Bass, 1974); Gordon Hearn, "Progress Toward an Holistic Conception of Social Work," pp. 63-71, and Donald E. Lathrope, "The General Systems Approach in Social Work Practice," pp. 45-62, in Hearn, ed., *The General Systems Approach: Contributions Toward an Holistic Conception of Social Work* (New York: Council on Social Work Educa-

tion, 1969); Ludwig von Bertalanffy, *General Systems Theory* (New York: George Braziller, 1968); and von Bertalanffy, "The Theory of Open Systems in Physics and Biology," in F.E. Emery, ed., *Systems Thinking* (Baltimore: Penguin Books, 1969), pp. 70-85. For a discussion of existential perspectives, see Rollo May, "The Contributions of Existential Psychotherapy," in May et al., eds., *Existence: A New Dimension in Psychiatry and Psychology* (New York: Basic Books, 1958) pp. 37-91.

13. For a discussion of culture's influence on behavior, see Robert A. LeVine, *Culture, Behavior and Personality* (Chicago: Aldine Publishing Co., 1973); and Clifford Geertz, *The Interpretation of Cultures* (New York: Basic Books, 1973). The conflict inherent in biculturalism is discussed by Christie W. Kiefer, *Changing Cultures, Changing Lives* (San Francisco: Jossey-Bass, 1974); and Federico Souflée, Jr., "Biculturalism: An Existential Phenomenon," in Ernesto Gomez and Roy E. Becker, eds., *Mexican American Language and Culture: Implications for Helping Professions* (San Antonio, Tex: Our Lady of the Lake University, 1979) pp. 18-39.

14. Sigmund Freud, *The Basic Writings of Sigmund Freud*, A.A. Brill, trans. (New York: Modern Library, 1938).

15. Joel Fischer, "Is Casework Effective? A Review," *Social Work*, 18 (January 1973), pp. 5-20.

16. Katherine M. Wood, "Casework Effectiveness: A New Look at the Research Evidence," *Social Work*, 23 (November 1978), pp. 437-458.

17. Mary Lee Smith, Gene V. Glass, and Thomas I. Miller, *The Benefits of Psychotherapy* (Baltimore: Johns Hopkins University Press, 1980), p. 33.

18. James Cross, "Can Casework Be Rational?" *Social Work*, 24 (May 1979), pp. 247-248.

19. Sigmund Freud, *Civilization and Its Discontents* (New York: W.W. Norton & Co., 1961), pp. 23-24.

20. Thomas Kuhn, *The Structure of Scientific Revolutions* (Chicago: University of Chicago Press, 1962), pp. 47-48.

# CHAPTER 7

# Chicago, Chicanos, and Mexicanos: A Community Perspective

## Albert Vazquez

C hicago is the fourth or fifth largest Hispanic city in the United States, which means that one of the largest concentrations of Hispanics in the United States exists in the state of Illinois. This article will describe the socioeconomic and political factors that influence the delivery of social services to Hispanics in the Midwest and, more specifically, in the metropolitan area of Chicago. It will outline existing mental health practice and education and their deficiencies as they relate to the communities of Mexicanos and Chicanos in Chicago's metropolitan area and will offer ideas for changes necessary to the development of more relevant services for Mexicanos and Chicanos. The term "Mexicanos" or "Mexicans" will be used to refer to Mexican nationals who reside in the United States but who are closely tied to Mexico and are influenced by and respond to political, social, and economic developments there. The term "Chicanos" will be used to refer to individuals who may be from Mexico or of Mexican descent and who reside in the United States, have become attached to this country, and are influenced by and respond to political, social, and economic developments here.

In the author's experience, the Mexicanos and Chicanos in the Chicago area can be described as predominantly Spanish speaking, with low incomes (average annual income, $9,500), and young (average age, 19 years). Most have large families. In background, they come from various socioeconomic levels and from both rural and urban areas, and they range in length of residency in this country from recent arrivals to those whose families have been here for three generations. Approximately three-quarters or more of the estimated two million Hispanics residing in the metropolitan area are of Mexican heritage. The growth of this population has lately resulted in the beginnings of exploitation of their economic buying power by established political and economic powers, such as corporations and the news media.

## Historical Background

Mexicanos started moving into the Chicago area in the early 1900s. Some came up in the migrant labor streams; some came on the railroads to work in the outlying areas in tanneries or in small towns. Most settled in Chicago around the railroads, steel mills, and stockyards, inheriting neighborhoods that once housed middle European or Mediterranean people. Each decade from 1940 until 1980 had periods of intensive migration. The migrations of the forties and fifties brought many Tejanos, people who had lived in Texas for several years before coming to Chicago. The sixties and seventies were periods when people came directly from Mexico because they either had friends or family in Chicago or because they knew that Chicago had a large Mexican population on which they could rely for established communal systems.

Three distinct Mexican communities developed in Chicago, each geographically separated from the others. One developed around the steel mills in South Chicago. Early migrants, mostly males, were used as strikebreakers in this area. During strikes in the thirties, company officials would hire them, ferry them into the mills from the lake side, house them inside the mills during the strike, and, when the strike was over, release them into the hostile community. Early accounts related the beatings of these strike breakers. Despite these problems, many Mexicanos and Tejanos began to move into South Chicago in the early forties because of the jobs then available in the steel mills. Two other smaller concentrations of Mexicanos developed around the stockyards (the community called the ''Back of the Yards'') and the railroad located toward the center of the city.

The Mexicanos inherited lower socioeconomic neighborhoods and with them the multiplicity of problems that plague such communities — bad housing, poor city services, rundown educational facilities, and a lack of recreational areas. Young people were initiated into existing gang structures, and a lack of skills training kept adult family members from retaining jobs in a manipulative economic system. Language barriers and an absence of education and job skills prevented most of the immigrants, especially those of the thirties, from making a stable transition to another socioeconomic level. Negative racial attitudes and prejudices also presented sometimes insurmountable obstacles to the socioeconomic development of individuals and families.

# Political Barriers

Despite their growing numbers, Hispanic immigrants in Chicago have not received any political representation by state or local government. Factors contributing to this have been and still are the geographic separation of the three Mexican communities, the high percentage of noncitizens and nonvoters in these communities, and the strong political machine that has effectively managed to keep out of power new groups coming into the city, other urbanized areas such as Aurora, Elgin, Peoria, and Joliet, and various suburban townships in Illinois. Hispanics represent 20 percent or more of the populations in each of the urban areas surrounding Chicago, yet they have little or no political representation in any part of the political structure.

Illinois politics present many problems for the development of social service delivery systems in general, but they offer an even greater obstacle to the development of delivery systems that have to incorporate linguistically and culturally unique populations. The dominant political system in the state can be more or less broken down into two distinct groups, the Democratic party, based in Chicago, and the Republican party, based in Springfield, the state capital. The federal government has recognized this division in the way it allots federal money to the city and state, which in turn determine their own priorities and utilization of the funds. The state government also recognizes the division by issuing block grants to Chicago for mental health services, thus allowing the city to determine its own priorities and develop its own delivery systems.

Unfortunately, both groups are equally unresponsive to the "new" minority groups, even though legislation has defined their obligation to provide services to the new residents. As a group, the Republicans are very conservative, often reactionary, and see new social developments as an encroachment on their liberties and way of life. Republicans in the state legislature recently introduced three bills that would have legislated a variety of regulations against undocumented workers. These bills verged on curtailing civil liberties for other segments of the population, such as those who employed undocumented workers, and were tinged with racist overtones. Although the Democrats make statements about helping the minorities, they in essence use social service money for their political programs.

# Mental Health Services

The brief description presented of the socioeconomic and political conditions in the Chicago area helps set the scene for explaining the current state of mental health practice in the area. Issues of service accessibility and the utilization of services by Mexicanos and Chicanos are linked to these conditions.

The Community Mental Health Centers Act of 1963 combined for the first time two service structures — state hospitals and community agencies — that had historically been separated by factors related to economics, social class, and definitions of deviant behavior. Psychiatric treatment (as opposed to psychiatric incarceration) would now be linked to a social treatment model for the poor that was epitomized by the settlement house movement of the late 1800s and early 1900s. Accessibility, community, and prevention were key concepts that were to be combined with an emphasis on psychiatry and deinstitutionalization. Then, in the late 1960s and the 1970s, attempts were made to develop comprehensive treatment centers responsive to the needs of particular "catchment areas," which were usually defined by political considerations rather than by knowledge of or regard for the populations to be served. At this time, use of a medical model was standard operating procedure, and physicians were administrators and final decision makers about the diagnosis and treatment of the "patient."

Federal dollars poured into medical and psychiatric institutions to develop new programs, and many state governments became involved by promising to pick up the tab as these funds faded out of the picture. Simultaneously, federal money was made available to educational institutions to train people to fill the positions opening up in the programs. Although the hiring and training of members of minority groups were emphasized, the federal government never really made this a criterion for allocating funds to these institutions. Consequently, few minority group members were recruited, a factor that helped create the current shortage of bilingual-bicultural, Spanish-speaking professionals.

## Accessibility and Utilization

Although the Chicago metropolitan area offers a multitude of mental health and social services to its population, few are used by Mexicanos or Chicanos or by any of the Hispanic groups residing there. Factors mentioned earlier come into play at the service entry level. One of the most important is politics, which affects accessibility and utilization beginning at City Hall. Specifically, the Illinois Department of Mental Health and Developmental Disabilities provides the city of Chicago with a block grant to operate sixteen to eighteen mental health centers. Through its central offices in City Hall, the city controls the hiring of individuals to work in these centers. Patronage is a key element in this process. (The author has been told by center directors that they had no control over the hiring of their staff.) This system has effectively kept out Mexicanos and Chicanos because they are not involved in the political system. Those who are involved are usually not qualified for the available jobs — although one sometimes sees unqualified *others* in these positions.

Even though they may speak English, few Mexicanos and Chicanos use the mental health centers. One major reason often cited by them is that they are not comfortable telling their problems to "Americans," who they feel do not understand them or their life conditions. Another is the embarrassment they experience when they have to resort to English to explain an emotion to the therapist and he or she cannot understand them. Monolingual Spanish-speaking people are left completely out of the picture at these centers, and if they happen to go there for services they will only be turned away without any attempt at intake or referral being made. Some city mental health centers sit in the heart of Mexican communities and do not service the Mexican population at all. In general, the experience of the author and others has shown that hiring bilingual-bicultural, Spanish-speaking workers increases the accessibility and utilization of any type of service center. This underlines the need to create training programs in mental health at the community level and to recruit bilingual-bicultural, Spanish-speaking individuals into professional schools.

Another political factor affecting the use of mental health services by Hispanics is the problem of who plans and determines priorities for funding and guidelines for implementation of services. When federal funds for community mental health began to dry up, the state set up a commission to develop a five-year state plan for mental health. This commission defined the mental health population to be served in terms of aftercare only, thus leaving out the Hispanic population in general, which is more prone to use emergency services, crisis management, and outpatient services as well as primary prevention programs geared to its socioeconomic needs.

## Educational Needs

Educational programs at the professional level in mental health and social services in the Chicago area rarely recruit Mexicanos and Chicanos. In addition, they have not developed curriculum relevant to understanding and working with this population. This can be seen by examining the programs offered by the professional schools. For example, in 1969, the University of Chicago's School of Social Service Administration had three Hispanic students (one Chicano) studying at the master's degree level. In 1980, five students of Hispanic origin were registered. The Jane Addams College of Social Work of the University of Illinois has not had more than four Hispanic students at any one time. Moreover, its curriculum of minority studies consists of one or two general survey courses that tend to focus on the black population. Few Hispanic instructors are recruited to teach in the schools, and none of those hired has tenure or a position of authority.

Given the "state of the art" of mental health services and education for Hispanics in Illinois (which the author fears may be similar in most of the midwestern states), we can hardly begin to document with any real clarity what services, if any, are effective with Chicanos and Mexicanos. Determining what really works is made all the more difficult because funding sources often define what programs must be operated and what modalities of treatment must be provided. Furthermore, a shortage of personnel limits the resources available: most Hispanic mental health professionals tend to come from Latin American countries. More specifically, many Hispanic psychiatrists are from a higher socioeconomic class than most Mexicanos and Chicanos and know little of the socioeconomic conditions to which these groups are subjected in the United States. Although they are Spanish speaking, this lack of knowledge compounded with their psychoanalytic medical training often limits their creativity regarding new approaches to treatment.

## Developing Relevant Services

Using experiences gained as a mental health worker and administrator, the author has determined that the following elements are necessary ingredients for establishing responsive mental health and social services for Mexicanos and Chicanos.

**Facilities.** Facilities should be comfortable, community based, and integrated both structurally and operationally with the rest of the community. At the beginning of the community mental health movement, storefronts were seen as the most viable setting for the delivery of services. However, their often run-down condition did not provide a very pleasant atmosphere for clients. The importance of the client's initial contact with the facility was later recognized, and more pleasant surroundings began to be envisioned by practitioners.

**Staff.** Staff members should be linguistically and culturally similar to the clients served. Being able to communicate in the client's primary language and having an understanding of his or her cultural values and morals can help put an already anxious individual at ease and also help prevent errors or problems from developing during initial contact and assessment. An example of such an error occurred when an Anglo Spanish-speaking therapist held an initial interview with a Mexican family and addressed the grandfather as *tú*, the familiar form of "you." As a result, the family did not cooperate during the interview and dropped out after that first contact. Experience indicates that match in social class is also an important variable in the communication between client and therapist.

In general, staffs should be flexible, able to meet with the client in less traditional ways, and have empathic feelings concerning the client's experiences. They should also have diagnostic skills based on an understanding of the client's social situation.

**Networks.** Therapeutic and social service programs must respond to the socioeconomic pressures experienced by clients. This means comprehensive linkages must be made with other services in order to develop a treatment plan that will help to alleviate the problems brought on by these pressures. For example, the symptom most often experienced by Mexicanos and Chicanos with whom the author works is deep depression, primarily brought on by a lack of socioeconomic resources.

**Political awareness.** Directors and administrators who are Mexicanos or Chicanos should be oriented toward politics, community development, and national and state economic growth and have a broad view of the parameters of mental health.

**Research.** There is a need for more conclusive data on mental health issues that concern Mexicanos and Chicanos. For instance, we need to know whether alcoholism and drinking patterns among Mexicanos and Chicanos are culturally influenced.

**Community-based training programs.** Training programs set up in the community should be linked up with existing community-based mental health programs and colleges for accreditation purposes. These types of programs have been very effective in the past. They help orient community residents to the social work profession and act as a feeder system to professional schools.

**Relevant curriculum.** Universities and colleges with BSW and MSW programs should develop curricula that encompass courses in mental health on issues relating to Hispanics. Such courses should focus on Mexicanos and Chicanos as together constituting the largest Hispanic group in the United States.

## Concerns for the Future

Analyzing the situation in the Midwest may help us focus on the extensive problems we face in developing responsive mental health programs for Mexicanos and Chicanos. Funding sources are drying up, although this may provide an incentive for innovation. We know that many treatment techniques commonly used in hospitals and community mental health centers are not effective with Hispanic clients in general, yet there is insufficient evaluative research data to document this. Clinical work with some types of families seems to be effective, but evaluative data are lacking on this topic as well. In the area of education, professional schools do not recruit Hispanics, nor do they pay attention to this population in the development of their curricula.

In general, politics plays a great role in determining mental health funding, planning, and implementation. What, then, is our role for the future? Mexicanos and Chicanos are a rapidly expanding population that is becoming more urbanized. It is therefore imperative that they become more involved in the political systems that influence legislative priorities for social services. In addition, they need to be trained as administrators, clinicians, and researchers and to be involved with curricula that help them work for the benefit of the Hispanic client. One way of helping would be to design community-based treatment modalities to take advantage of the tendency of Hispanics to participate in communal activity.

Finally, we need to focus on and exploit the resources within our community and within our constituency. As a group, Mexicanos and Chicanos have enormous inner strengths. They work hard, are upwardly mobile, and are extremely adaptive, given the opportunity. Social service models focusing on these strengths may have a greater rate of success than those focusing on weaknesses symptomatic of a social condition that stifles individual initiative and creativity.

# CHAPTER 8

# The Therapist as Social Change Agent

## Josie Torralba Romero

*T*he model about to be described is based on the premise that for any culturally sensitive method of treatment to be implemented and effective, it must first be acknowledged and its validity recognized by the hierarchical powers that be within the mental health system. At present, the only generally acceptable model of treatment is the medical model. This dominant model within the community mental health system allows little or no flexibility to address *Raza* mental health needs in a culturally sound manner.* The author will not analyze that structure here but will refer to a few striking examples to illustrate this.

From its entry into the system, a *Raza* family comes up against procedures that are at once unfamiliar and offensive. The separation of service units is an instance of the service system's lack of relevance for *Raza* families. Almost from the time a family walks through the door, its members are separated and directed to various units, one for children, another for adults, and still another for the elderly. The lack of bilingual-bicultural staff in the units is an additional barrier. After a cold and impersonal process that requires the client to divulge personal information first to a clerk and then to an intake worker, he or she is finally assigned a therapist. After that comes the famous "fifty-minute hour," which is particularly distasteful to Chicanos because of its shortness and the clear emphasis it places on rigid limits. These qualities hamper the natural process of establishing *confianza* and prevent the parties involved from taking the time to share social amenities. The overall focus on "time as money" that is basic to the Protestant ethic in general undermines the values Chicanos place on quality of time and relationships.[1] These are only a few of the obstacles that Chicanos encounter when they seek help within the mental

---

*The translation of this and other Spanish words can be found in the glossary at the end of this book.

health system, and they are impositions contrary to the cultural values of *Raza*.

Can a *Raza* therapist begin to remove some of these obstacles within the system and introduce cultural relevance? The answer is yes. Can the therapist maintain his or her job and sanity in the process? Again, the answer is yes. However, the therapist must be able to analyze the system, document needs and changes, have a support system of colleagues and organizations, and be active in the community in order to obtain its support. Above all, the therapist must be unwilling to sacrifice social work principles despite pressure.

# Factors Affecting Intervention

This article presents a practice model in which the therapist is also a social change agent. Use of the model enables *Raza* social workers to clarify their roles as therapists within their community. The model combines a psychocultural-social orientation with strong advocacy aimed at changing the system. In using this or any model, workers should be mindful of crucial elements that may govern clients' acceptance or rejection of treatment and services. As a result of working with Chicanos, recent immigrants, and migrant farm workers, the author has identified various factors that affect the therapeutic process. A discussion of these factors and their incorporation into the therapeutic approach is presented as a prerequisite to understanding the therapist–social change agent model. Briefly, these factors include culture and language, the acculturation process, concepts of family roles, social conditions, and the therapist's attitudes and skills. Sensitivity and sociocultural understanding can help the therapist make use of these elements and convert them into effective tools.

## Culture and Language

It is important for therapists to understand cultural factors such as language and other communication symbols, the role of the support system, and spiritual beliefs and values in order to interact with *Raza* populations. The practitioner or educator must be able to ascertain the degree of importance that such elements play within the individual and each family unit. The level of acculturation and assimilation within each individual family member varies and must be assessed to develop a unique understanding of the person and the situation. To do so, it is very important to comprehend the value *Raza* places on the concepts of *confianza* ("trust"), *respeto* ("respect"), *vergüenza* ("shame"), and *orgullo* ("pride"). Appropriate attention to cultural elements such as these can provide the practitioner with effective tools for culturally relevant therapeutic approaches. Too often the system does not allow the flexibility to incorporate these elements into the delivery of services. For example, with the existing intake process it is difficult to establish *confianza*, but this is a crucial step because it will influence the client's acceptance or rejection of services. Although establishing *confianza* varies with the individual, those approaches most acceptable to Hispanics presume the establishment of rapport through informal discussions of topics of common, everyday events or comments on objects at hand. *Confianza* is strengthened through the sharing of personal experiences relevant to the current situation. A direct, respectful approach aids its development.

*Respeto* must also be conveyed by the therapist. *Respeto* can be demonstrated by using *usted* when addressing any adult at first meeting and until familiarity has been established, all older persons, and groups. The formal term for "you," *usted* communicates a sense of respect and transcends the social class and professional affiliation or background of the persons involved. In addition, respect can be shown by an expression of concern for the whole family's health, welfare, or situation. The therapist can also convey it in many nonverbal ways, from the tone of voice and style of dress adopted to the acceptance of social amenities such as a cup of coffee, a soft drink, or food.

A sincere effort by the mental health professional to obtain a clear *conocimiento* of the Hispanic's value system and ways of responding to problems and the professional's attempt to identify problems through an open attitude will strike a responsive chord among *Raza*, who are receptive to expressions of recognition and acknowledgment regarding the importance of the family. *Conocimiento* can be attained through listening and observing with a bilingual-bicultural orientation. It can provide vital insights into the Hispanic family's community and cultural ties and the impact of these ties on the lives of family members. On too many occasions, professionals make assumptions about authority roles without accepting or understanding and respecting the family's own decision-making processes. Therefore, the need for culturally specific training is crucial if relevant, high-quality therapeutic services are to be delivered.

Careful cultivation of Spanish-language skills further allows the professional to recognize both verbal and nonverbal clues. The expression of "feeling words" — Spanish words used to express emotions, such as *triste*, and love and caring for human beings —together with nonverbal gestures may be a tool of maximum importance in the educational or therapeutic process. This does not mean to imply that non-Spanish-speaking individuals, whether they be *Raza* or Anglo professionals, cannot work effectively with Hispanics, but rather that to be effective the intervention effort must include bilingualism as an integral part of the overall strategy. The language needs of the client or the community are a key variable in providing services to Hispanics, and the provider team must have some members proficient in Spanish, particularly when a large segment of the community to be approached does not speak English. A keen sense of timing for using Spanish-speaking staff is also critical. Staffing patterns should reflect the community served.

The cultural concepts of *orgullo* and *vergüenza* have meanings that go beyond pride and shame. They are seen as personal qualities that are measurable through actions and are demonstrated through exercising or not exercising self-control in difficult situations. Any sign of weakness is seen as shameful. *Orgullo* is highly regarded and respected by the family and community. This makes it very difficult for some *Raza* families to accept and use direct clinical services. Therefore, the system must offer complementary preventive, educational, and outreach services to reach the segment of the population that ascribes to these values.

## Acculturation

Cross-cultural researchers point out that immigration to a new country reflects the search for an improved lifestyle brought on by a lack of personal fulfillment in the old environment.[2] *Raza* in this country, whether foreign or native born, are historically linked to this quest. Immigrants have by necessity worked their way up the American socioeconomic ladder by to some extent adapting to or identifying with the values and lifestyle of the dominant culture. For Chicanos, this has frequently meant negating or suppressing their identity and culture. Difficulties in adapting to the conflicting values of two cultural systems result in increasing psychological stress and eventual behavioral dysfunction.[3] The process of acculturation has two facets: physical acculturation and psychological acculturation. Groves emphasizes that psychological acculturation brings changes in the individual's "world view."[4] These include changes in the norms governing interpersonal behavior and in the adoption of a sense of fatalism and a future time perspective.

For Chicanos, the degree of acculturation can generally be viewed in terms of a continuum from "Mexican" to "American." During acculturation, a narrowing of cultural distance takes place from the gradual change in the *Raza* person's world view to the normative world view of the dominant social group (that is, from the movement of Chicanos toward the adoption of the value orientation of Anglo American middle-class norms). Researchers have not yet provided concrete methods for specifically assessing acculturation levels among Chicanos. Castro uses the terms "high," "medium," and "low" to assign degrees of acculturation.[5] Therapists should consider and understand the emerging sociocultural acculturation patterns, which reflect real differences in lifestyle and life needs and utilize them to plan the most appropriate intervention approach. A meaningful psychotherapeutic approach with a low-income client may not be a psychoanalytic approach but rather a reality-based, action-oriented process of finding him or her a job or housing. Appropriate therapy can be provided during this process if the therapist has a respectful understanding of the client's environment and addresses the client's immediate needs.

It is important for the therapist to understand the client's concept of mental and physical health. Depending on their degree of acculturation, Chicanos may have a perspective on mental health that is on the continuum somewhere between the institutionalized view of the dominant culture and the indigenous folk-medicine views of rural Mexicans.[6] Through an understanding of basic cultural elements, the therapist can formulate a therapeutic approach that will make sense to the client. When the client is "highly" acculturated, he or she may accept traditional psychotherapy as a treatment modality; those of "low" acculturation may not see psychotherapy as curative and may end treatment early unless it is modified to include cultural factors that make sense to them. The therapist and the system must be flexible to adopt different approaches.

## Concepts of Family Roles

For a therapist, understanding the client's family structure and the role of each member in it provides significant information for the therapeutic process. When the family's natural coping mechanisms are understood from a cultural perspective, it facilitates their use in therapy. The family, nuclear or extended, plays an important role in the life of Chicanos. The individual's contact with his or her immediate or extended family can help reduce anxiety in stressful situations but can be a source of anxiety at other times. Family dynamics can better be addressed when observed in the family's natural setting. Therefore, home visits and outreach by professional staff are important components of a delivery system. This point is often overlooked when agencies discourage professional staff from making visits to clients' homes.

The immigrant family's initial experience in the United States is characterized by culture "shock" and by encounters with language barriers and different cultural traditions, values, beliefs, and lifestyles. For many it will be the first time they have experienced racial discrimination or been confronted with different institutional systems. Many also have not previously been exposed to an urban setting, having come from rural agrarian environments. The adjustment to these different experiences produces tremendous stresses and pressures on families. The therapist must be aware of inherent stress factors to help clients understand their situation.

## Social Conditions

It is the belief of this author that the majority of mental health problems exhibited by Chicanos are not pathological. Rather, they result from a combination of socioeconomic stresses that are compounded by poverty, racism, oppression, lack of access to educational and legal systems and institutions as well as to health care, and the experience of acculturation and culture shock.

Therefore, in order for the therapist to intervene effectively, he or she must not only obtain extensive knowledge about the client's experiences but must also address the stress-producing factors as well. The treatment plan must include action-oriented goals.

## Therapist's Attitudes and Skills

The therapist's attitudes and skills are determining factors in achieving successful therapeutic results. It is the therapist's responsibility to his or her client to have an accurate working knowledge of the client's cultural background and life experience. In addition, he or she must be culturally self-aware, that is, understand his or her own individual and collective group attitudes or feelings relative to culture. Therapeutic skills can be mastered on an intellectual level, but the most important factor is integrating these skills into the delivery of services.

It is the therapist's responsibility to clarify the client's expectations of treatment.[7] Therapist and client are partners in the development of the treatment plan and its implementation, and the client is expected to carry out the assignments that coincide with his or her treatment expectations. Clients must understand in every step of the process that success depends on their active participation in treatment. This can only happen when they have accepted major responsibility for their own treatment and the therapist has consistently clarified his or her own role in the process.

It is essential that the therapist be sensitive and aware. This sensitivity and caring can be used in favor of social change when the client is taught to take a more active role in his or her treatment and in the furtherance of the community's well-being.

## Social Change Model

The cultural factors and treatment approaches already described address critical concepts to be understood by the practitioner. The treatment approaches and modalities that can be derived from them are many. However, incorporating them into the existing structure of the mental health system is not easy. Some of the reasons have been alluded to, such as the prevailing system's insistence on the fifty-minute hour, the intake process, the assigned role of the therapist, and other institutional policies that do not allow flexibility. Top and middle management rarely include *Raza* professionals, a situation that has direct impact on the degree of support culturally relevant treatment modalities receive.

The barriers to the use of mental health services by Chicanos are many.[8] The therapist–social change agent model is based on the premise that if culturally relevant treatment modalities for *Raza* are to be accepted and incorporated into the present mental health delivery system, the *Raza* therapist must work to confront institutional racism and to develop community power through culturally relevant community education. The therapist's role has to be redefined to include simultaneous involvement in several areas. In addition to working with the *familia*, the therapist who is a social change agent must be involved in networks such as coalitions, advocacy groups, and *Raza* organizations, community organizations such as church and self-help groups, political systems such as government on all levels and appointed boards, public information and education systems such as newspapers and community forums, and bureaucratic institutions such as mental health and social service agencies and the criminal justice system.

When *Raza* social workers enter the present service delivery system, they clash almost immediately with the prevailing service structure. One example that most of us have seen is that of an eager young *Raza* social worker employed in a community mental health center. He or she arrives with new ideas for programs or services based on his or her own knowledge and life experiences. The first confrontation occurs when the immediate supervisor questions the worker's rationale for a proposed activity or therapeutic process. The supervisor tells the worker that the activity does not fit in with the goals and objectives of the unit and that besides, there are no funds to cover such activities. If the worker insists on following through with the proposed activity or process, he or she is cited for insubordination and is told that continuing to disregard the supervisor's recommendations means the loss of a job.

Unfortunately, scenes like this happen too frequently. This writer has seen *Raza* therapists become bitter, frustrated, and discouraged by having to work with complex bureaucratic regulations that have no significance in the day-to-day process of providing services to the Spanish-speaking community and stifle workers' creativity and ability to deliver culturally appropriate services. As a result, some workers choose to "blend in" to escape the direct and indirect pressures from the system.

How can the conscientious *Raza* therapist overcome the barriers he or she faces within the agency? We know of the importance of natural support systems within the family. Likewise, the therapist needs a network of colleagues and organizations through which he or she receives support, disseminates information, and promotes advocacy efforts. These networks also can be used to share professional knowledge, increase therapeutic skills, and thereby improve service methodologies and delivery. They are particularly important for those who work in isolated centers without other *Raza* professionals.

In order to be aware of the current needs of the community, the therapist must be involved in some grass-roots organizations that address basic needs. Self-help organizations are clues to what and where the needs are, and involvement in such organizations provides the therapist with firsthand information. Before there can be any *confianza* between the *Raza* therapist and the community, the therapist has to be an active participant in the community's activities. Also, education and information must flow to and from the community. The information the therapist receives from the community is invaluable for planning strategies for social change and may be used to apply pressure to the system.

The impact of politics in the field of mental health cannot be ignored or avoided. Given this reality, the therapist must become involved at the local, state, and national level. Appointment to various task forces provides access to the development of policies and procedures designed to meet the needs of *Raza* and other underserved populations. In California the state government usually controls about 90 percent of all funds for local community mental health centers, and therapists in that state therefore need to know which legislators play an important role in deciding on funding and then have to maintain frequent contact with them. Education of these key people is necessary in order to have an impact on future legislation related to mental health services for *Raza* and other ethnic communities. In general, the therapist who is an agent for social change must be familiar with the entire gamut of political mechanisms and use the media and formal organizations to mobilize public scrutiny of political and bureaucratic systems or to educate and inform the general public or special target groups. However, the appropriate time to bring issues into the political arena must be well thought out.

When preparing to use the media, the therapist must plan the timing carefully and have documented data to substantiate significant points. Television can be made use of through public service announcements or interviews on community interest programs, as can local radio programs in which issues are discussed. Newspaper articles or letters to the editor that focus on issues and problems can also educate and inform the public. A particular issue can be covered simultaneously through radio, television, newspapers, and other means and thereby reach a broader audience. This is important because a well-informed public can provide the support necessary to generate public pressure.

The therapist–social change agent must expose institutional racism, subtle or overt, through education. Stereotypical attitudes held by the dominant society contribute to inadequate and irrelevant service delivery. This means starting within the agency so that all staff can address the mental health needs of *Raza*. Sensitizing administrative and clinical staff promotes an understanding of Chicanos and thereby slightly weakens institutional racism. Mental health centers can provide in-service training to staff from educational institutions and governmental agencies and in doing so make those institutions a little more accessible and relevant to the Hispanic population. Working with other bureaucracies must be preceded by work within the therapist's own bureaucracy. No organization will bring about changes of a higher level than the change it allows within its own structure and among its own staff.[9]

Eventually, simultaneous involvement by therapists in clinical work and advocacy for social change will create pressure on the system and force it to allow innovative programs. The therapist–social change agent model emphasizes commitment to relevant services and commitment to the need for institutional change.

If it is successful, the Hispanic client and the community will have access to relevant, high-quality, mental health services, and the system will be doing what it is paid to do. *Si se puede!*

## Notes and References

1. *See* Max Weber, *The Protestant Ethic* and *The Spirit of Capitalism*, Talcott Parsons, trans. (New York: Charles Scribner's Sons, 1958).

2. See M.E. Spiro, "Culture and Personality: The Natural History of a False Dichotomy," *Psychiatry* (1951), pp. 14 and 19-46.

3. Henrik Blum, *Planning for Health: Development and Application of Social Change Theory* (New York: Human Sciences Press, 1974).

4. J. Groves, as cited in Felipe Castro, "Levels of Acculturation and Related Considerations in Psychotherapy with Spanish Speaking-Spanish Surname Clients,"

Occasional Paper No. 3 (Los Angeles, Calif.: Spanish Speaking Mental Health Research Center, University of California, 1977).

5. Ibid.

6. Nelba Chavez, "Mexican Americans' Expectations of Treatment, Role of Self and of Therapists: Effects on Utilization of Mental Health Services," in Patricia Preciado Martin, ed., *La Frontera Perspective* (Tucson, Ariz.: La Frontera, Inc., 1979).

7. Josie T. Romero, "Health-Mental Health Promotion Strategies: Hispanic Natural Support Systems," in Ramon Valle and William Vega, eds., *Hispanic Support Systems* (Sacramento, Calif.: Department of Mental Health, State of California, 1980).

8. Marta Sotomayor, "Mexican-American Interaction with Social Systems," *Social Casework*, 52 (May 1971), pp. 316-322.

9. Romero, op. cit.; and Arturo Chevali Arroyo et al., "Street Psychiatry: A New Approach to Community Mental Health." Paper presented at the Fifth Meeting of the Pan American Forum for the Study of Adolescence, West Conference, San Francisco, Calif., Feb. 1-4, 1979.

# CHAPTER 9

# The San Antonio Model: A Culture-Oriented Approach

## Ernesto Gomez

*H*uman service literature relating to service delivery for Chicanos points to the need for considering language and culture as significant variables in the provision of mental health services.[1] In addition, the 1978 report by the task force on the mental health of Hispanic Americans of President Carter's Commission on Mental Health, which contains the most comprehensive description to date of the mental health status and needs of Hispanics, emphasizes the need for developing culture-specific models of service delivery to address the culturally based needs of Hispanics.[2]

The "state of the art" of developing culture-specific models of intervention is sound. This article discusses one such model, known as the San Antonio Model (SAM). After the theory behind SAM was formulated and the model itself was field-tested, a four-year study examining its effectiveness, directed by the author, was conducted as part of its continued development. The sample consisted of twenty-nine clients who were Chicanos and were associated with the outpatient services offered at two community mental health centers in San Antonio, Texas. Clinical symptoms, target complaints, and service satisfaction were used as outcome measures.[3] The findings, which are considered tentative because of the limitations of the study, have shown that SAM is significantly ($p<.05$) associated with clients' improvement in severity of clinical symptoms and target complaints as well as with a high level of clients' satisfaction with services. The design of the study and its findings are to be reported at another time. The present article will be devoted to presenting a description, albeit abbreviated, of SAM. However, first a review of the thinking on which the model is based is in order.

# Approach to Model Building

SAM was developed as part of the work associated with a project funded by the National Institute of Mental Health and operating under the auspices of the Worden School of Social Service, Our Lady of the Lake University of San Antonio.[4] This specialized project was designed to develop a culture-oriented model of service delivery and to respond to the need for professionally trained social workers capable of providing culturally compatible mental health services to Chicanos. The approach to the development of SAM that was adopted by the faculty involved in the project was characterized by five major concerns.

First, a review of existing models of intervention revealed sophisticated theoretical and technological conceptualizations. The limitations of existing models generally rested in their inability to integrate a consideration of the client's culture into the helping process. Despite this serious shortcoming, the project's staff recognized that the basic principles of helping and the general tenets of practice formulated would certainly be of value in working with all clients and should be built on in newer formulations of practice.

Thus, rather than starting from scratch, we examined a number of existing models in search of a theoretical framework that reflected the basic core of social work practice and could be adapted for specific application with Chicanos. We looked for models that incorporated the impact of environmental stresses on people and that allowed for cultural pluralism among clients. That is, we were interested in models that addressed the concept of the "social" as well as the "individual." This is particularly important in working with Chicanos in light of the findings of several studies suggesting that environmental stresses associated with minority status, migration, acculturation, and poverty contribute to an individual's vulnerability to emotional disturbances.[5] The effects that culture has on behavior and its significance in the helping relationship have been documented by many social scientists.[6] Models subscribing to cultural pluralism were desirable because they would allow the infusion of a culture-oriented perspective of practice.

Second, we wished to develop a model of practice that could be used with clients belonging to different ethnic and racial groups. Our thrust was not to develop a model for practice only with Chicanos, but one that would be oriented to the culture of the client, whatever that culture might be.

Third, we wanted to develop a model that was simple, cost-effective, and lent itself to use by practitioners. This meant that although our model had to be conceptually sound, it also had to be straightforward in its application.

Fourth, our approach to developing SAM was to formulate practice techniques that allowed the worker to acquire information on the cultural configuration of each client. Because Chicanos are culturally heterogeneous and it is extremely important to guard against stereotyping them, we did not consider it feasible to attempt to produce a comprehensive description and complete understanding of the culture of Chicanos. In our approach we focused on conceptualizing practice theory rather than on attempting to describe that culture. The approach emphasizes the development of practice knowledge and skills appropriate for infusing cultural factors into the helping situation. The worker is not required to have an in-depth knowledge of Chicanos' culture even though general sensitivity to it is essential. Basically, the client is viewed as the expert on his or her individual culture and is thus expected to contribute culture-related data. The worker's task, we maintain, is to facilitate the client's sharing of this data.

Fifth, we disagreed with statements asserting that social casework is ineffective, which thereby make the task of developing culture-oriented models of practice impossible. Fischer's examinations of studies on the effectiveness of casework did not reveal that casework is ineffective but that the few studies conducted suffered from a lack of sound research design and methodology.[7] The social work profession has yet to conduct sound evaluative research on the effectiveness of social casework. Hence, questions remain as to the effectiveness of various casework models.

With these concerns in mind, we chose to adapt the mediation or interactionist model developed by Schwartz and Shulman.[8] SAM builds on the mediation model's practice theory by incorporating several culture-oriented helping strategies that are designed for application with Chicanos. Thus, SAM focuses on the cultural characteristics affecting the client's behavior and problem.

## View of Practice

As is the case with the mediation model, SAM is different from models of social work practice based on the belief that "an outside expert can help people with their problems by deciding beforehand what their desired states of being should be and then enlisting clients in an effort to achieve them."[9] Instead, SAM reflects the view that a client with certain tasks to perform and a professional with a specific function to carry out engage each other as interdependent actors in a system. It emphasizes experience and effect, step-by-step processes, and situational rather than structural descriptions of people in difficulty.[10]

This particular view of social work practice is marked by four major assumptions. Schwartz suggests that social work's function is most powerfully expressed when it directs itself not to the individual or to the social but to the relationship between the two and when it is concerned with "those energies that flow in both directions between people and their institutions; . . . the reaching, and pressuring and straining that goes on between them as both strive to carry out their sense of need and purpose."[11] The worker views the client not in static terms with pathology attributed to the client, but with an emphasis on how the client interacts with others and how he or she relates to important systems. This viewpoint maintains that it is impossible to understand the behavior of clients without recognizing how their behavior is affected by the behavior of others.[12]

The mediation approach also assumes a "symbiotic" model of human relationship in which people and their important environmental systems are interdependent, "each needing the other for its own life and growth, and each reaching out to the other with all the strength it can command at a given moment."[13] In the interactionist framework, "system" refers to any entity residing outside the client, such as family, friends, or job.

A third major assumption is that both the individual and the systems contain within them the strength and potential to build a common ground for interacting. People and systems are viewed as being able to act in their own interest without being bound by their past experiences.[14]

The fourth assumption is of the ever-present possibility for what Schwartz terms "symbiotic diffusion," which can block or obscure the mutual dependence between person and system. Such a breakdown in the symbiotic relationship is introduced by the complexity of situations, by divergent needs, or by the difficulty involved in communication. Recognizing that complex systems contain an unequal distribution of power, which affects relationships, Schwartz maintains that a force is needed to guard the symbiotic striving and continue the interaction between people when each party is tempted to dismiss the other as unreachable.[15]

Schwartz has stated that the function of social work is

to mediate the transactions between the people and the various systems through which they carry out their relationships with society — the family, the peer group, the social agency, the neighborhood, the school, the job, and others. The mediating skills are designed to create not harmony but interaction, based on a sense of strength, feeling, and purpose, drawing on the often all-but-forgotten stake of people in their own institutions, and of the institutions in the people they are meant to serve.[16]

In the mediation model as presented by Schwartz, there is constant movement by the client (individual or group) toward its system and by the system (group, agency, family, school, or others) toward its member or client. The social worker encourages interaction or mediation between them, with the focus being not on conciliation but on realistic exchange, based on the realities of the situation and the actual business between the client and the system.[17] As is the case with many other models of practice, the mediation model makes a passing reference to the need to consider the culture of the client, but it fails to discuss the question of cultural relevance, much less provide the practitioner with direction on incorporating the client's cultural configuration into the helping process.

## Theoretical Base

SAM has adopted Schwartz's theoretical framework of practice, which is in direct contradiction to the positivist model in which the independent worker-subject acts on a client-object from a distance to understand, change, or mend the client, using standards drawn from the worker's own special frame of reference. Schwartz believes that the paradigm of study-diagnosis-treatment, which social work adopted from medicine, research, and positivist science, is at odds with what actually happens between the worker and the client.[18] In formulating the knowledge base for the mediation model, Schwartz drew from various theoreticians who made contributions to the interactionist construct. Dewey's interactionist view of the teaching-learning process and Follett's work on experience as the powerhouse that generates purpose, will, thought, and ideas both served to shape the model.[19] Another theoretician contributing to the reciprocal construct was Buber, in his work on reciprocal language, the I-it versus I-thou formulations, and explorations of the "dialogical" character of human relations in which he delineated the central theme of the reciprocal approach to the helping process. It was Buber who stated that "only in partnership can my being be perceived as an existing whole."[20]

The theoretical base of SAM is shaped primarily by two interrelated social and theoretical frameworks: symbolic interactionism and culture. Symbolic interactionism was first developed by Mead and later elaborated on by a number of theoreticians.[21] Blumer identifies three fundamental premises on which symbolic interactionism rests: (1) human beings act toward things on the basis of the meanings the things have for them, (2) the meaning of such things is derived from the social interactions the individual has with other people, and (3) these meanings are modified through an interpretative process used by the individual in dealing with the things encountered.[22]

Blumer points out that in psychology and social science today, there is the tendency to take the meaning something may have for the individual for granted and "to treat human behavior as the product of various factors that play upon human beings; concern is with the behavior and with the factors regarded as producing [it]."[23] The meaning of things is ignored or bypassed, the result being merely identification of the initiating factors and the resulting behavior. Blumer maintains that ignoring the meaning of things toward which people react is in effect a falsification of the behavior under examination.

In contrast, Blumer himself sees meaning "as rising in the process of interaction between people .... Thus, symbolic interactionism sees meaning as social products, as creations that are formed in and through the defining activities of people as they interact."[24] In addition, he states that people's actions are built up through a process of self-indication, a "communicative process in which the individual notes things, assesses them, gives them a meaning, and decides to act on the basis of the meaning."[25] Overall, human interaction is seen as emergent, negotiated, and often unpredictable. It is symbolic in that it involves the manipulation of symbols, words, meaning, and languages.

Thus, in SAM we assume that the perspectives of both client and nonclients involved with a problem must be taken into consideration if an "objective common ground" is to develop.[26] The literature on social work practice with Chicanos suggests that the worker's efforts need to be aimed at identifying the client's unique perspective or meaning given to things.[27] This perspective or meaning refers to the linguistic and symbolic aspects relevant to the culture of Chicanos, which social workers must relate to in order to understand clients who are Chicanos. But symbolic interactionism goes beyond the client's perspective. It also applies to the perspectives of the system and the worker. The system is related to the client and worker through the process of self-indication. Likewise, workers relate to the system and to clients on the basis of the meaning associated with them. SAM assumes that the perspectives of clients, nonclients, and workers need to be taken into consideration if meaningful interaction is to take place. It further suggests that the perspective of each can be modified through social interaction.

## Emphasis on Culture

The second essential theoretical construct associated with SAM is the concept of "culture." Culture is frequently referred to but rarely defined in social work literature. Divergent definitions of culture are presented in social science literature, but social work has not yet adopted one that fits its particular need. A review of definitions of culture conducted by Kroeber and Kluckhohn indicates that such definitions vary from those of a high level of abstraction to those of great concreteness.[28] The former type of definition is so general that it fails to identify real-life characteristics. The latter type is so specific that practitioners would find it difficult to remember all its facets.[29] However, a definition formulated by Kluckhohn was cited by Pollak as being particularly useful and appropriate for social work because it included the aspect of feeling. Kluckhohn's definition is as follows: "Culture is the composite of the specific ways of thinking, feeling, and acting which differentiates one group (or person) from another."[30]

In this definition, the ways of thinking refer to traditional ideas and attitudes, the ways of feeling refer to the values or effects attached to traditional ideas, and the ways of acting refer to behavior associated with the ideas and values. The definition is particularly interesting because it echoes symbolic interactionism theory. That is, the ways of thinking and feeling mentioned coincide with the assessment and assignment of meaning to things in symbolic interaction. Self-indication, then, is a vehicle through which culture is expressed. A person notes things, assesses them through the use of traditional ideas and attitudes, assigns meanings to them that reflect values and effects associated with such thinking, and then translates those meanings and feelings into behavior.

Combining the elements of assessment and assignment of meaning into what we will call a "culture screen," we can conclude that people process stimuli through this screen, from which behavior is formulated. Rather than make blanket statements about the culture of any given client group and risk stereotyping and generalizations, we can define culture as the manner of thinking, feeling, and acting that represents what is regarded as the individual's cultural makeup. The culture screen determines the meaning assigned to things, which results in behavior.

The culture screen is in operation not only with clients but with workers and systems as well. Workers and systems employ their culture screens in formulating the interaction they will have with clients and with each other. Whenever major cultural differences or conflicts are present in any facet of the client-worker-system triad, attention is usually focused on mediating between the different cultural structures. The old saying that the self is the worker's primary tool in any helping intervention underscores the idea that no human intercourse is without the influence of culture. Carrying this point one step further, we can say that the client and the system also rely on the use of "self" for all interactions.

Another essential element of the consideration of culture reflected in SAM is that in the practice of social work we are not concerned with the totality of the culture of the client or system. Time constraints do not allow it, and it is not necessary to our work. Rather, we are concerned with those cultural elements that have a relationship to or a bearing on the problems we deal with in social work. If elements of the client's or system's culture do not relate to the concern being addressed, we do not need to consider them. Our perspective on culture is more specifically focused than that of sociology or anthropology, and it is concerned with those elements of culture that either contribute to a problem or serve as a resource in dealing with the problem. The relationship between the client's culture and the problem being addressed has been conceptualized as a cultural assessment model in an earlier discussion.[31] There it is indicated that in classifying cultural features as contributors to a problem or resources for solving it, the worker is not judging the inherent value or desirability of cultural features but is stating the manner in which they affect the problem. The key operating assumptions of the cultural assessment model are the following:

1. Helping interventions with Chicanos must make use of the unique elements of the culture that have a major influence on behavior.

2. The cultural diversity among Chicanos requires individualized consideration of clients' cultural configurations (that is, thinking, feelings, and actions).

3. The worker's interest is in those cultural features that have a bearing on the client's problem.

4. Whether belonging to the client or the system, cultural factors can be either detrimental to people's social functioning or can serve as a viable resource in dealing with people's problems.

5. The worker brings his or her own culture to the helping relationship.

6. Casework is in itself a manifestation of culture. Its practices and principles are derived from and are an integral part of culture.

7. The client is the most knowledgeable person about his or her particular cultural configuration and as such is the best source for learning about the culture.

## The Helping Process

With this theoretical orientation and set of assumptions in mind, the worker is ready to begin the helping process. The entire helping transaction and each separate interview are in general conceived of as having a beginning, middle, and an end. Schwartz described four phases in the helping process, and these have been expanded in SAM to include a culture-oriented dimension of practice.[32]

The four phases of work in the mediation model are tuning in, beginnings, work, and transitions and endings. In the tuning-in phase the worker prepares to meet the client and to be sensitive to indirect cues about concerns the client may find difficult to discuss.[33] The worker considers potential themes of concern as well as the client's possible initial reactions to him or her as well as to the agency. The thrust behind this preparatory phase of work is the sensitization of the worker, who will as a result have a better chance of reading the client's indirect messages.

The chief task in the beginnings phase is to clarify purposes and roles. This is done in the early sessions with the client, in which the worker explains the agency's services and a working contract—an agreement that connects the agency's service with the client's sense of felt need—is set up. The importance of this phase rests on two assumptions: (1) until the client is clear about the purpose of the work, the interaction between worker and client will be marked by prolonged indirect testing and (2) the client must be actively involved in working on that part of his or her agenda that relates to the agency's service.

In the work phase, the worker and client together focus on the areas of concern identified in the contract. Each has his or her own sense of function and task, but in this phase a premium is placed on the worker's ability to determine the client's themes of concern, help the client elaborate on these themes as well as keep his or her discussions rooted in reality by dealing with associated effects, and present the client with a continuous demand for work. The work phase is extremely complex. Typical behaviors of the worker during this phase include contracting, elaborating on the client's concerns, providing empathic responses, sharing feelings, demanding work, identifying obstacles, providing data, and dealing with systems.

Transitions and endings involve the special dynamics related to ending the client-worker relationship. Worker behaviors typical of this phase include helping the client assess what he or she has learned and express honest feelings about ending the relationship, sharing feelings with the client about the helping process and the ending of the relationship, and attempting to help the client use the sense of urgency usually associated with ending to produce effective work.

## Culture Tuning In

In SAM, the phases of the helping process just described are complemented and modified by a culture-oriented dimension. This dimension consists of the following four features: culture tuning in, culture inquiry-study, cultural assessment, and the culture check. Theoretically, culture tuning in serves as a subphase of the tuning-in phase, while the remaining culture-oriented features complement the beginnings phase of the mediation model.

The culture tuning-in subphase is designed to focus attention on the cultural variables that may be present in the client's situation. The intent is that the worker visualize the cultural context of the client's situation and be sensitive to the forthcoming encounter with a client participating in the Mexican American culture.

## Culture Inquiry-Study

The culture inquiry-study feature is designed to focus attention on the client's linguistic and cultural practices that may relate to or be affected by the problem presented. Just as the social worker normally asks clarifying questions about the applicant's problem, personality, and situation, he or she now gives special attention to linguistic and cultural variables operating in the client's life. In addition, the worker will inquire about the cultural makeup of the client's environment.

The thinking through of the possible effects that the identified cultural features have on the problem takes place during this time. In concentrating on this, the worker can tentatively begin to categorize the cultural features in accordance with their relationship to the problem. At this point, the worker may need to seek additional information to help him or her understand the cultural forces operating in the case. It is important to emphasize that these postulated relationships and subsequent groupings of cultural features are tentative. This will be the worker's initial attempt to identify the significance, if in fact there is any, that these cultural characteristics hold for the helping process.

The information obtained from this inquiry will give the worker additional material for conducting the preliminary assessment and negotiating pertinent intervention. The inquiry process will be helpful in communicating to the client that his or her linguistic and cultural practices are important and will be given attention. The process can be of further use in communicating to the client that the worker cares about those aspects of his or her life situation that on the surface may not appear to be related to the presenting problem.

Five tasks have been identified for the worker to perform in this feature of practice. These are to acquaint the client with the culture-oriented approach, conduct a language settlement, inquire about cultural variables, reflect on the cultural variables identified, and consult resources on the meaning of the cultural indicators detected. The language settlement task has been fully developed and discussed elsewhere.[34] In brief, it is a process in which the social worker and client explore and select the language most appropriate for use in the helping process. The worker alone cannot make assumptions about the language Chicanos need or prefer in the helping situation.

Because the client and social worker have language needs or preferences that may or may not be complementary, joint exploration of these needs and preferences is necessary before the client and worker can go beyond the initial phase of their interaction. The primary focus in language settlement is to make social workers' communications linguistically compatible with the language needs of clients who are Chicanos. The client-centered nature of the settlement requires the worker to assume primary responsibility for an appropriate response to clients' assessed language needs. This response can take one of two forms. The worker can either adapt to the client's language needs or preferences or can refer the client to another worker who has the necessary language skills for providing professional service. Language settlement interviews include the use of generally accepted interviewing techniques. It is crucial for the client to know that he or she is to be a participant in this phase of the helping process and that his or her thinking and feelings are important.

## Cultural Assessment

Cultural assessment has been described elsewhere as a tool for organizing the worker's thinking regarding those aspects of the client's cultural configuration that have a relation to the problem being addressed.[35] In undertaking this assessment, the worker is not particularly interested in the traditional anthropological definition of culture but is concerned with those elements of culture that influence or manifest themselves in the client's behavior or in environmental forces.

Cultural assessments are conducted in three parts. The first involves organizing cultural influences through the use of the Cultural Assessment Grid; the second is an analytic statement that synthesizes the dynamics of the case at hand; and the third is the identification of alternate sets of intervention strategies. The Cultural Assessment Grid shown in Figure 1 provides the practitioner with a framework for analyzing the cultural features relevant to the helping process. On the "Cultural Factors" plane of the grid are the cultural features belonging to the client and the cultural features that are part of the environment with which the client interacts. On the "Relationship to Focus of Concern" plane are cultural features that contribute to the problem being addressed and resources for dealing with the problem. The grid organizes these four dimensions into four possible types of cultural features. Type 1, client-held features that could be resources for dealing with problems, might include the concept of respect or motherhood or the high value placed on families. Environmental resources, Type 2, could include extended-family mutual-aid support systems or other supportive organizations and institutions. Type 3, client-held features contributing to the problem at hand, could include such beliefs as Chicanos should not speak English, Chicanos are less intelligent than Anglos, or the female's place is strictly in the home. Type 4, negative aspects of the environment, could include racism, certain religious dictates, and institutional policies.

The arrows in the grid indicate the relationships of these features. They suggest that the worker should be able to find a corresponding environmental dimension for each of the client-held cultural features and vice versa.

The second feature of the cultural assessment is an analytic statement that combines the inferences and judgments derived from the application of the Cultural Assessment Grid. This statement resembles that of the force field model developed by Lewin.[36] It calls for a summation of the cultural features that serve as impediments to social functioning and of the cultural aspects that serve as resources in problem resolution.

In examining cultural features that contribute to the problem, the worker is interested first in determining if the client suffers from cultural confusion. Cultural confusion occurs when a person attempts to accommodate contradicting sets of values or dictates from the "Mexican" and "American" cultures. Souflée states that cultural confusion occurs when a person cannot associate a definite norm with an appropriate context.[37] According to Kiefer, "This confusion arises in either of two circumstances; when more than one definitive norm seems to be

## Figure 1.

## Cultural Assessment Grid

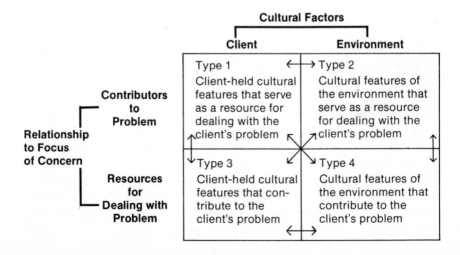

applicable at once (multiple norms) or when experience contradicts a person's assumptions about what is expected of him (normlessness)."[38]

Second, the worker is concerned with identifying possible cultural conflicts between the client and other people or social systems. These generally include conflicts that result from generational gaps, conflicts between the client and people of other cultures, and conflicts between the culture and institutional policies.

The final step in the cultural assessment is a listing of several sets of intervention approaches that specifically indicate the relationship of the interventions to the problem and to the culture of the client and the environment. The worker will use these in negotiating a service contract with the client. What is crucial here is that the worker must be able to explain the influence the case's cultural factors had in determining the proposed strategies and justify the strategies in terms of these cultural factors. Overall, cultural assessments may be summarized by indicating that the single most important factor is the worker's willingness to involve the client in identifying and making judgments about the cultural factors involved in the situation. This author and Rivas have reviewed the process in the following way:

> Individuality and the emphasis on clients' perceptions of their life situations and cultural reality help guard against the application of cultural stereotypes and worker biases. The cultural assessment framework presented here is intended to serve as an adjunct to whatever assessment or diagnostic model is employed by practitioners. It requires that the worker specifically discuss culturally-oriented behaviors and classify them in terms of "contributors" to the problem or as "resources" for working with the problem. Additionally, workers are asked to identify cultural dictates and assess these in terms of degree of synthesis or conflict. Behavior should be explained in terms of what might be causing it to be defined as conflict.[39]

## Culture Check

The culture check reflects the belief that the client is the most knowledgeable person concerning his or her culture. It therefore involves the worker in taking a reading of the client's feelings and perception of the helping process. The sole purpose of the culture check is to verify the worker's assessment, proposed service alternatives, and projected outcomes of service by soliciting the client's views on their compatibility with his or her culture.[40] The worker's principal interest is to check his or her assessment and understanding of the client's situation with the client's perception of his or her own cultural reality. Confirmation of or disagreement with the worker's perceptions will help yield a greater understanding of these areas of the service process by the worker and the client.

# Perfecting the Model

The task of developing a culture-oriented approach to intervention was a challenge but an exhilarating experience as well. Our work in this regard was prompted by the apparent need for practice approaches that systematically incorporate a consideration of clients' culture into the helping process. SAM is firmly rooted in the frameworks of symbolic interactionism and culture, both of which promise to have a significant effect on social work's perspective on human behavior and approach to intervention.

The simultaneous use of the mediation model and the culture-oriented practice dimension can result in a greater understanding of the client and his or her cultural environment. The hypothesis that the complementary features of this model and practice dimension and their specialized focus on culture result in the provision of effective services to Chicanos is supported by our research. Although the research findings are considered to be tentative because of the limitations of the study, they suggest the impact that SAM had on clients who were Chicanos. Future analyses of the data will be concerned with determining the practice techniques associated with SAM's effective results. This endeavor will identify areas of conceptualization that need improvement or modification. In effect, the overall thrust of the research will be toward model building that focuses on the continued refinement of the current conceptualization of SAM.

## Notes and References

1. See Guadalupe Gibson, Ernesto Gomez, and Yolanda Santos, "Bilingual-Bicultural Service for the Barrio," *Social Welfare Forum, 1973* (New York: Columbia University Press, 1974); Amado M. Padilla and Rene A. Ruiz, *Latino Mental Health: A Review of the Literature* (Washington, D.C.: U.S. Government Printing Office, 1976); and Juliette Ruiz, ed., *Chicano Task Force Report* (New York: Council on Social Work Education, 1973).

2. *The President's Commission on Mental Health: Task Panel Reports,* Vol. 3 (Washington, D.C.: U.S. Government Printing Office, 1978).

3. For a discussion of the type of measurements used, see the following sources: for clinical symptoms, Leonard R. Deronatis, *The SCL-90 Scoring, Administration and Procedures Manual I* (Baltimore, Md.: Johns Hopkins University School of Medicine, 1977); for target complaints, C.C. Battles et al., "Target Complaints as Criteria of Improvement," *American Journal of Psychotherapy,* 20 (1966), pp. 184-192; and for satisfaction, D.L. Larsen et al., "Assessment of Client/Patient Satisfaction: Development of a General Scale," *Education and Program Planning,* 2 (1979), pp. 197-207.

4. The special project through which the model was developed was supported by Grant No. T01-MH-13619 awarded by the Social Work Training Branch of the National Institute of Mental Health.

5. See E.B. Brody, "Migration and Adaptation: The Nature of the Problem," *American Behavioral Scientist*, 13 (1969), pp. 5-13; F. Hashmi, "Immigrants and Emotional Stress," *Proceedings of the Royal Society of Medicine*, 63 (1970), pp. 631-632; and Danuta Mostwin, "Uprootment and Anxiety," *International Journal of Mental Health*, 5 (Summer, 1976).

6. See Harry C. Triandis and Richard W. Brislin, eds., *Handbook on Cross-Cultural Psychology*, Vol. 5: *Social Psychology* (Boston: Allyn & Bacon, 1980); Marvin K. Opler, *Culture and Social Psychiatry* (New York: Atherton Press, 1967); and Alfred R. Lindesmith and Anselm L. Strauss, *Social Psychology* (New York: Holt, Rinehart & Winston, 1949).

7. Joel Fischer, "Is Casework Effective? A Review," *Social Work*, 18 (January 1973), pp. 5-20; and Fischer, ed., *The Effectiveness of Social Casework* (Springfield, Ill.: Charles C Thomas, Publisher, 1976).

8. See William Schwartz, "Between Client and System: The Mediating Function," in Robert W. Roberts and Helen Northen, eds., *Theories of Social Work with Groups* (New York: Columbia University Press, 1976); and Lawrence Shulman, "A Study of Practice Skills," *Social Work*, 23 (July 1978), pp. 274-280.

9. William Schwartz, "Social Group Work: The Interactionist Approach," *Encyclopedia of Social Work* (New York: National Association of Social Workers, 1971), p. 1256.

10. Ibid.

11. Schwartz, "Between Client and System: The Mediating Function," p. 183.

12. Lawrence Shulman, *The Skills of Helping Individuals and Groups* (Itasca, Ill.: F.E. Peacock Publishers, 1979).

13. William Schwartz, "The Social Worker in the Group," *Social Welfare Forum, 1961* (New York: Columbia University Press, 1961), p. 155.

14. Shulman, *The Skills of Helping Individuals and Groups*.

15. Schwartz, "Between Client and System: The Mediating Function."

16. Ibid., pp. 183-184.

17. Ibid., pp. 184-185.

18. Ibid., p. 175.

19. See John Dewey, *Democracy and Education: An Introduction to the Philosophy of Education* (New York: Macmillan Publishing Co., 1916); and Mary P. Follett, *Creative Experience* (New York: Longmans Green, 1930).

20. See Martin Buber, *I and Thou* (New York: Charles Scribner's Sons, 1958); and Buber, "The William Alanson White Memorial Lectures (Fourth Series)," *Psychiatry*, 20 (May 1957), p. 106.

21. See George H. Mead, *Mind, Self and Society* (Chicago: University of Chicago Press, 1934); H. Blumer, *Symbolic Interactionism: Perspective and Method* (Englewood Cliffs, N.J.: Prentice-Hall, 1969); Blumer, "Society As Symbolic Interaction," in Jerome G. Manis and Bernard N. Meltzer, eds., *Symbolic Interaction: A Reader in Social Psychology* (Boston: Allyn & Bacon, 1978); R. Collins, *Conflict Sociology* (New York: Academic Press, 1975); and Manis and Meltzer, eds., *Symbolic Interaction: A Reader in Social Psychology*.

22. Blumer, *Symbolic Interactionism: Perspective and Method.*

23. Ibid., pp. 2-3.

24. Ibid., pp. 4-5.

25. Blumer, "Society As Symbolic Interaction," p. 98.

26. See Shulman, *The Skills of Helping Individuals and Groups.*

27. See Ernesto Gomez and Karen Cook, *Chicano Culture and Mental Health: Trees in Search of a Forest* (San Antonio, Tex.: Our Lady of the Lake University, 1978); Gibson, Gomez, and Santos, op. cit.; and Federico Souflée, Jr., "Biculturalism: An Existential Phenomenon," in Gomez and Roy E. Becker, eds., *Mexican American Language and Culture: Implications for Helping Professions* (San Antonio, Tex.: Our Lady of the Lake University, 1979).

28. A.L. Kroeber and Clyde Kluckhohn, "Culture: A Critical Review of Concepts and Definitions," *Papers of the Peabody Museum of American Archaeology and Ethnology,* 47 (1952).

29. O. Pollak, "Cultural Dynamics in Casework," in Cora Kasius, ed., *Social Casework in the Fifties* (New York: Family Service Association of America, 1964).

30. Kluckhohn, as cited in ibid., p. 84. See also Clyde Kluckhohn, *Mirror for Man* (New York: McGraw-Hill Book Co., 1949).

31. Ernesto Gomez, "Cultural Assessment: A Think Paper." Unpublished manuscript, San Antonio, Tex., 1978.

32. Schwartz, "Between Client and System: The Mediating Function."

33. Lawrence Shulman, *A Study of the Helping Process* (Vancouver, B.C., Canada: School of Social Work, University of British Columbia, 1977).

34. Ernesto Gomez, "Language Settlement in the Social Work Process: Chicano Culture and Mental Health," Monograph 3. Unpublished manuscript, San Antonio, Tex., 1978.

35. Gomez, "Cultural Assessment: A Think Paper."

36. Kurt Lewin, *Resolving Social Conflicts* (New York: Harper & Row, 1948).

37. Souflée, op. cit.

38. C.W. Kiefer, *Changing Cultures, Changing Lives* (San Francisco: Jossey-Bass, 1974), p. 133.

39. Ernesto Gomez and C.E. Rivas, "Chicano Language and Culture: Implications for Human Services," in Gomez and Becker, eds., *Mexican American Language and Culture: Implications for Helping Professions,* p. 69.

40. Ernesto Gomez, "The Gomez Model for Bilingual-Bicultural Intervention with Chicanos." Unpublished manuscript, San Antonio, Tex., 1978.

# *Summation*

# CHAPTER 10

# A State of the Art Analysis

## Ismael Dieppa

*T*he event from which the foregoing articles were drawn—the "Mental Health Education and Practice for Chicanos and the Mexican American Community: A 'State of the Art' Workshop"—was an occasion for the delivery of diverse, scholarly, and stimulating papers. The presentations ranged from historical, ideological, theoretical perspectives to models of social work training and practice with Chicanos and the Mexican American community. They reflected the extensive efforts made by Chicano and Chicana academicians and practitioners during the seventies to find models of training and practice relevant to their communities. Although these models emerged from the pragmatic experiences of the authors, they highlight the need for an ideological perspective on social work with Chicanos as the *raison d'être* of social services in Mexican American communities.

In order to do justice to the entire workshop and offer a description of the "state of the art," the following format was developed for this analytic summation. The first three papers were classified as a conceptual framework providing historical, ideological, and theoretical perspectives from which the six papers exploring the state of the art in the areas of training and practice could be reviewed. Because the six papers presented a range of models in these areas, they were classified accordingly. Thus, this writer approached the definition of the state of the art from two perspectives: that of a conceptual or theoretical framework, and that of training and practice "models." The resulting summation also includes a critique of the training and practice models and examines the implications of the workshop for the future.

## Historical Overview

Gallegos's opening paper presented a historical perspective on social work education and Chicanos during the sixties and seventies. He viewed this period as one of accomplishments for Chicanos in social work education. Gallegos analyzed the progress made by Chicanos within the context of the concept of a "cultural variable" and examined this unifying theme in the three interrelated areas of social work education, mental health, and social work education of Chicanos.

The cultural variable evolved in the early 1900s as a key concept of the movement for cultural pluralism that accompanied the advent of the settlement houses and the imperative to assimilate and Americanize immigrants. Gallegos posited that systems theory and other social perspectives in the 1960s brought the concept of culture as one important variable in social work practice and mental health intervention to the fore again.

Although the settlement movement seemed to advance the concept of cultural pluralism during the social reform period (1900-20), its goal in relation to the masses of poor immigrants who arrived in this country was assimilation. Consequently, the advent of psychoanalytic theory in the 1920s and its acceptance and adoption by social workers resulted in a loss of concern for issues related to cultural pluralism. From the 1930s to the 1950s the social work profession focused its knowledge and efforts on the intrapsychic aspects of human problems. The failure of ethnic minorities of color to assimilate was perceived as resulting from their own failings. Observing that social work practice and education were dominated by psychoanalytic theory, Gallegos concluded that social work education was tied both ideologically and conceptually to a monocultural, dominant community. Nevertheless, the civil rights movement of the fifties and the War on Poverty of the sixties renewed social and political interest in pluralism, and minorities of color began to envision broader life choices and opportunities.

The concept of culture as a factor in understanding ethnic and racial minorities and racial inequality once more became an important factor in social work education and practice. Gallegos traced this development in terms of the efforts of the Council on Social Work Education (CSWE), the National Institute of Mental Health (NIMH), and schools of social work in response to the activism of Chicano and Chicana social work leaders. These efforts included the adoption by CSWE of Accreditation Standard 1234A and the establishment of several minority task forces and projects. Special training programs funded by NIMH were geared to the recruitment and education of social workers from ethnic and racial minorities for practice in mental health. Gallegos concluded that the attempts made by schools of social work to develop minority courses using a historical context and content on cross-cultural methods were inadequate. In spite of the efforts just described, after 1975 there was a downward trend in the enrollment of minority students in schools of social work. This erosion has been completed by the elimination of federal funding for mental health training.

According to Gallegos, the most significant advances over the past ten years for Chicanos in social work came in the area of curriculum development. These accomplishments were facilitated by an alliance between forces in social work education and the field of mental health and the interests of Chicanos in social work and mental health. However, Gallegos concluded by questioning the present validity of such an alliance. He pointed out that although the alliance helped establish the culture of Chicanos as an important variable, it has not answered the question of "to what end?" He summed up the present situation by suggesting that empowerment is the only relevant goal of intervention for Chicanos and their communities.

## Importance of Ideology

The paper by Atencio on ideology in social work strives to respond to Gallegos's question of to what end are we involved in social work education and practice. A question posed by Atencio at the workshop provides a conceptual linkage to Gallegos's historical perspective: Can *la Raza** survive despite social services? Or can *la Raza* live without them?"

Like Gallegos, Atencio presented a historical perspective. However, his analysis of the four stages of the evolution of social work focused on the economic foundations of capitalism in the United States and the ideological base that supports it. Although social work did not have an ideology of its own, its direction emanated from the socioeconomic conditions, the structures and social patterns, and, above all, the predominant domain of ideas and values that ultimately influence social patterns.

Atencio drew a parallel between the historical evolution of social work and the Mexican American experience in terms of the economic foundations, social patterns, ideas, values, and ideology that emerged from the interaction of the factors described. In his view, the social work profession grew out of the early Progressive movement in the United States and was informed by ideology based on the values of Protestant Anglo America. He described the Progressivists as the religious and professional people of the emerging business class during the early industrialization period whose goal was social control and the improvement of social functioning and who sought to use the social sciences to identify the causes of social problems and rationalize the administration of charities and corrections.

---

*The translation of this and other Spanish words can be found in the glossary at the end of this book.

Changes in the economic foundation of the country as a result of the Great Depression (1929-40) and World War II and shifts in international power brought pressure for changes in the predominant society's values and goals. The civil rights movement and Great Society programs raised the consciousness of the poor and oppressed minorities. According to Atencio, the experience of Chicanos in this country also evolved from economic foundations and social patterns, in this case colonial status and the poverty precipitated by the American conquest of the Mexican territories in the Southwest. This colonial status persisted through the 1930s, until World War II opened new routes of geographic and social mobility.

By the 1960s, a movement among Chicanos to affirm their identity had emerged. Alternative values based on the myth of Aztlan gave birth to a new consciousness. Chicanos saw themselves as an "internal colony," subjected to economic exploitation and underclass status.

Although Atencio did not analyze clearly the relationship between the social work profession and the emergence of Chicanos' new ideology, he stated that Chicanos questioned the dominant Anglo American ideology as they struggled to change the infrastructure. He perceived social work as operating under the guidance of the values of the dominant society. His historical analysis of the evolution of social work leads the reader to the conclusion that the profession continued to be captive to societal values that stressed a social control function, despite its response to the trends of the sixties favoring reform, advocacy, and community action.

Atencio suggested that these trends required an adjustment from social work in the form of new knowledge and new methods. He also stated that the emerging ideology of Chicanos has implications for social work theory and practice. His discussion raises many provocative questions for the reader: What is the nature of the new knowledge and the new methods? To what extent are social services provided within the framework of Chicanos' ideology? To what end are Chicanos involved in social work education and practice? To what extent does the ideology of Chicanos justify the professional actions of Chicano and Chicana social work practitioners? Do the ideology of Chicanos and the nature of social work practice in communities of Chicanos directly reflect socioeconomic realities?

Both Gallegos and Atencio presented the response of social work to Chicanos as an evolutionary process intricately related to the dominant ideological pattern of society and the theoretical perspective used to resolve social problems. However, while Gallegos saw the attention given to culture in mental health intervention as a historical anchor point in the achievement of Chicanos in social work education and practice, Atencio perceived the progress made so far as the result of a growing consciousness (*conscientización*) among Chicanos, an affirmation of their historical and sociocultural (Indian) roots that gave birth to a "Chicano movement." This movement sought to change the internal colonial status of Chicanos and the infrastructure that has kept them on the periphery since 1848. It should be noted that Gallegos and Atencio concluded that empowerment should be the "end" within the framework of the emerging ideological stance. However, for both of them, a critical question lingers in search of an answer: Can *la Raza* survive despite social services, or can *la Raza* live without them?

## Criteria for Practice

The third paper in the trilogy of conceptual perspectives explored criteria for evaluating approaches to social work practice. In this discussion Bounous's treatise will be reviewed within the context of the presentations by Gallegos and Atencio and be seen as a logical link to the six training and practice models that followed it.

Bounous proposed that criteria relating to two areas of concern are essential in evaluating or building practice approaches. These areas are the knowledge base and the value base of social work practice. In focusing on the knowledge base, Bounous indicated that the criteria used to assess the knowledge base concern its power.

It might be added parenthetically that both Gallegos and Atencio address Bounous's points indirectly. Gallegos identified the cultural variable as an essential aspect of the knowledge base for practice with Chicanos. On the other hand, Atencio argued that the function of social work with Chicanos can be best understood or explicated in terms of both the dominant values of the society from which the profession derives its direction and the emerging ideology of Chicanos.

Bounous viewed knowledge as a source of power that enables one to predict and control one's environment. He considered concepts as "the building blocks of practice theory" that are fundamental to the formulation and evaluation of practice approaches. He proposed five levels of conceptual understanding: Level 1—Naming or identifying all the basic concepts in the real world, Level 2—Copresence, or the association of two concepts in place and time, Level 3—Covariation, or concomitant variation of two variables or concepts, Level 4—Sequence, or the use of time as a variable, and Level 5—Causality. Overall, Bounous presented what he considered to be a fundamental and traditional social work perspective: that the interconnectedness of individual to group to culture, from past through present to future, attributed to systems theory in the sixties and early seventies and now to the ecological perspective, has existed in social work thinking for at least seven decades. Thus, he advanced both a multiple cause problem analysis and a multiple intervention approach to the development of practice.

Although the propositions advanced by Bounous could be applicable to the development and analysis of social work practice approaches, they seem to reflect an inherent contradiction. If, as he stated, his view of interconnecting, circular, and cumulative effects in problem solving has been the traditional social work thinking for at least seven decades, and if it has been effective in practice, why have Gallegos and Atencio and other authors questioned its efficacy in minority communities? Bounous's propositions seem to place an undue emphasis on knowledge and its power to effect creative change. However, as Atencio contends, the power of ideology, by which he means values, goals, and purpose, cannot be ignored, because it directs the use of knowledge to the advantage of a dominant group at the expense of subordinated populations such as ethnic and racial minorities. In addition, knowledge from sociology, psychology, and social work has been used to explicate the ethos of ethnic and racial minorities within an ethnopathological framework. Sociocultural and psychological theoretical analyses have frequently placed causative factors and solutions within the context of the individual and familial psyche. Why has a profession that views life, behavior, and social problems within the context of an ecological or systems theory (which should include culture as a significant element) focused its goals, priorities, and resources on a "mental health solution" to the problems of oppressed populations? It should be noted that Gallegos suggested that one of the most important accomplishments in social work education in the last decade was the establishment of the culture of Chicanos as a variable in research and intervention. However, his concluding remarks defined empowerment as the only relevant goal of intervention for Chicanos and their communities.

## Training and Practice Models

The six training and practice models can be analyzed in terms of the questions raised in the preceding section of this article. Table 1 provides a summary of the models, which were classified according to the three categories of practice-training, practice-research, and practice. Within these three categories the theoretical base, focus of practice, target populations, and research findings for each model were identified. The sequence of the following analysis of the papers will follow their categorization in the table.

# Table 1.

# Models for Training and Practice, by Category

| Practice-Training | Practice-Research | Practice |
|---|---|---|
| Minority Human Service and Training Program (Saenz) | Bicultural Treatment Framework (Souflée) | Cross-cultural and Cross-ethnic Assessment (Silva) |
| *Theoretical base:* psychosocial, eclectic approach based on personality theories. | *Theoretical base:* eclectic, ecosystem approach. | *Theoretical base:* systems theory and theories of multiple causation and psychosocial dynamics. |
| *Focus:* traditional therapeutic modalities with humanistic perspective and advocacy. Emphasis on both practice and training. | *Focus:* environmental manipulation and individual change and provision of direct services. | *Focus:* a framework for assessment based on the factors of human behavior, culture, and ethnicity. |
| *Target population:* Hispanics and other minorities. | *Target population:* Chicanos | *Target population:* minorities. |
| *Research findings:* no research design in progress. However, evaluative research has been performed. | *Research findings:* not provided; research in progress. | *Research findings:* no research in progress. |
| | San Antonio Model (Gomez) | Therapist as a Social Change Agent (Romero) |
| | *Theoretical base:* interactionist model and culture-oriented concepts. | *Theoretical base:* psychocultural-social orientation, with an emphasis on advocacy and systems change. |
| | *Focus:* the individual and the environment and cultural pluralism. | *Focus:* the implementation of a cultural approach within a psychosocial framework, with the therapist functioning as an agent for social change. |
| | *Target population:* clients of every background. | *Target population:* Chicanos. |
| | *Research findings:* model tentatively associated with improvement in clinical symptoms and target complaints and with clients' satisfaction with services, as a result of findings completed after the workshop and based on work with twenty-nine clients; further research planned. | *Research findings:* no research in progress. |
| | | Community Perspective (Vazquez) |
| | | *Theoretical base:* community mental health perspective, combined with sociocultural elements and political advocacy. |
| | | *Focus:* therapeutic services based on cultural and linguistic congruence between client and worker. |
| | | *Target population:* Chicanos and Mexicans. |
| | | *Research findings:* no research in progress. |

## Community-Based Efforts

The paper presented by Saenz on community-based services and training described a psychosocial approach to the provision of mental health services to a minority population, more specifically, to Hispanics in Utah. The theoretical underpinnings were defined in terms of an emphasis on the promotion of the individual's best functioning within his or her own reality.

Most of the paper was devoted to a detailed description of a community-based program that functions within the framework of a traditional mental health center offering three basic components: outreach services, partial hospitalization, and aftercare. The methods of intervention range from individual, group, and family conjoint therapy to consultation, training, and the operation of recreational and resocialization groups.

This model demonstrates the feasibility of developing a mental health service program oriented toward ethnic minorities and using a psychosocial approach within the context of a traditional agency. Although the training aspect of the program is not described in detail, it is clear that it is provided through a professional and paraprofessional internship program and other training and consultation activities. However, it is not clear to what extent, given the traditional nature of the mental health center, the ethnic and cultural aspects of the problems of Hispanics and other minorities are given a significant emphasis in actual intervention approaches. Are nonminority, monolingual (that is, Anglo) staff provided training in relation to the language and sociocultural and psychological attributes of Hispanic clients? Is there any measure or assessment of the effectiveness of traditional intervention modalities with Hispanics? Does the approach actually place a greater emphasis on community development and social action as a mental health intervention strategy than on the traditional clinical modalities? These questions were not addressed specifically in this paper. Consequently, the reader does not reach a clear appreciation of the model in action. However, this training project received the National Council of Community Mental Health Centers' award for minority service and training.

## Effectiveness of Practice

The papers by Souflée and Gomez are classifiable as practice-research models. Both authors reported on social work intervention models that at the time were in the process of being tested through a research-demonstration project format.

Souflée began by posing a number of searching questions. How can effective social work practice models for Chicanos be developed in the absence of effective social work practice models? Can models be identified and adapted for effective social work with Chicanos? How can this technology be bilingualized and biculturalized and then be expected to be any more effective with Chicanos than it is with Anglos?

While not attempting to answer the questions he posed, Souflée actually gave a rhetorical and seemingly conflicting response. He views social work as incapable of bringing about social change. Social workers, he argued, should do what they have been trained to do best: provide direct services to clients in an attempt to alleviate their suffering and pain. However, the model he proposed is based on a definition of social work practice as the purposeful engagement between worker and client in the joint resolution of internal and external problems.

If, as Souflée indicated, social work technology can be assailed because of its empirically untestable effectiveness, how can he propose an eclectic multidimensional model for practice with Chicanos that is based on the same technology and knowledge base he attacks? Is his model that of practice limited to an ameliorative function primarily aimed at easing clients' suffering and pain, or, as he described later, focused on environmental manipulation through advocacy and resource mobilization and on individual change?

Lack of a detailed description and analysis of the proposed model prevents the reader from developing a clear picture of the Bicultural Treatment Framework with which Souflée worked. Because the research was in progress, data were not available to provide a clearer definition of the model and its effectiveness.

Souflée's conclusion could be stated in terms of a question that would bring us back to the ideological inquiries raised by Gallegos and Atencio — To what end social work for Chicanos? Or, can la Raza survive despite social services, or can la Raza live without them? Can we talk about the state of the art of social work with Chicanos without first examining the state of the art of social work practice?

## A Culture-Oriented Model

In his paper on the San Antonio Model, Gomez reported on a field-tested, culture-oriented model based on a theoretical framework reflecting the basic core of social work practice and adapted for specific application with Chicanos. However, he claimed that its emphasis was not on developing a model for practice with Chicanos, but on developing a model that would be oriented to the culture of the client whatever that culture might be. This contention must be understood within the context of the author's statement that language and culture are two significant variables in the provision of mental health services to Chicanos. There is a dilemma inherent in a conceptual model that attempts to be both universal (applicable to any client's culture) and specific (applicable to particular linguistic and cultural attributes of Chicanos). In light of the absence of tested midrange theoretical frameworks in social work practice in general, and specifically of those addressing the experience of Chicanos, the author's universal approach does not seem to be tenable. The dilemma is compounded, as Souflée stated, by the empirically untestable effectiveness of social work.

The San Antonio Model is an adaptation of the mediation or interactionist model developed by Schwartz and Shulman.[1] Gomez incorporated into the model culture-oriented strategies for application with clients who are Chicanos. It seems to this writer that many Chicanos and other minority practitioners use this strategy of adapting existing theoretical frameworks by incorporating culture-oriented elements.

The model assumes the following: (1) social work practice is most powerful when addressed to the relationship between the individual and the social, (2) there is a symbiotic and interdependent relationship between people and their environment, and (3) both individual and system contain within themselves the strength and potential to build grounds for interaction.

Gomez noted Schwartz's theory that individuals have a stake in their institutions and institutions have a stake in those they serve. However, this theoretical construct fails to take into account the fact that oppressed people who have been objects of institutional racism and rejection do not have a claim on oppressive societal institutions. These institutions are not "theirs." On the other hand, the institutions may not have a stake in ethnic and racial minorities and their status. The allegiance of the institutions is to the dominant population that controls them and for whom they were created. Because, as suggested by Atencio, institutions are a creation of the ethos of a people, reflecting their culture, values, goals, and ideologies, the institutions tend to be alien to ethnic and racial minorities. Thus, if Gomez's model is adapted from Schwartz's theoretical framework of practice, there would seem to be a conflict or incompatibility regarding its application to and use with Chicanos and other minority populations.

Gomez assumed that the conjoint application of the mediation model and culture-oriented practice dimensions can provide for the continuing interplay of the practice feature within the two and result in a greater understanding of the client and his or her cultural environment. He concluded that the San Antonio Model remains a conceptual description with tentative indications of effective results with clients, based on a limited sample consisting of twenty-nine people. His further research efforts may throw light on Souflée's query as to how we can take social work, bilingualize and biculturalize it, and expect it to be more effective with Chicanos than it is with Anglos.

## Focus on Assessment

Silva presented a discussion of cross-cultural and cross-ethnic considerations that was an assessment and not an intervention model. She described this approach as providing a framework for organizing assessment steps in a process that identifies effective means of intervention. According to her, it provides a way to collect cultural and ethnic data. The model focuses on three major concepts: human behavior, culture, and ethnicity. Sets of variables are described for each of the concepts. Silva contended that the model uses a systems approach to theory that advocates multiple causation principles and evaluation of both the internal and external forces that affect people.

Although Silva identified a number of important theoretical concepts and suggested that her approach is a holistic one applying systems theory, the reader is left with the impression that the model itself is missing. That is to say, the listing of concepts and variables are not connected conceptually as a model that may provide a systematic approach for the understanding and prediction of cross-cultural and cross-ethnic behavior. The framework she proposed provides a scheme by which a set of concepts may be applied in the assessment of clients. Perhaps the brevity of the paper did not do justice to the powerful concepts used by Silva as the theoretical foundation for her assessment approach.

## The Therapist and Social Change

The last two papers emerged from the authors' experiences as mental health practitioners providing services to Chicanos. In her paper on the therapist as social change agent, Romero viewed the medical model as too constricting to address *Raza* mental health needs in a culturally sound manner. Her model stresses a combination of psychocultural-social orientation with a strong advocacy role.

Romero identified a number of crucial elements in working with Chicanos: culture and language, the acculturation process, concepts of family roles, social conditions, and the therapist's attitudes and skills. Her practice model includes cultural approaches that incorporate the following concepts: language and communication symbols such as concepts of *confianza* ("trust"), *respeto* ("respect"), *vergüenza* ("shame"), and *orgullo* ("pride"), the role of the support system, and spiritual beliefs and values. Unlike Souflée, Gomez, Saenz, and Silva, Romero argued for culturally specific training. In contrast, Gomez indicated that the worker, in his model, need not have in in-depth knowledge of the culture of Chicanos.

One of Romero's basic premises is that the majority of mental health problems exhibited by Chicanos are not pathological in nature but are a result of a combination of socioeconomic stresses compounded by poverty, racism, oppression, lack of access to educational and legal systems and institutions, lack of health care, and acculturation and culture-shock experiences. She also believes that it is the responsibility of the therapist to have accurate knowledge of the client's cultural background and life experience. Of all the authors reviewed here, she articulated the strongest position for culture-specific knowledge on the part of the social worker if he or she is going to be effective in work with Chicanos.

Romero is unique in her definition of the role of the social worker or therapist as a social change agent whose concern goes beyond the problem presented by the client. She defines this role in terms of involvement with networks, community organizations, political systems, public information and education systems, and bureaucratic institutions.

## The Midwest

The paper by Vazquez did not present a specific practice or training model as such. However, Vazquez made positive recommendations for the development of mental health services to Chicanos with particular reference to the Midwest. He analyzed the lack of Chicano and Chicana social workers and mental health services among Chicanos in Chicago in terms of the socioeconomic plight of Chicanos and their exclusion from the political system. He concurred with Romero by noting that a lack of socioeconomic resources is the most important cause of depression and mental health problems among Chicanos who are clients with whom he works.

Drawing on his experience in Chicago, Vazquez recommended a community-based mental health approach integrated both culturally and operationally with the rest of the community. He indicated that staff should have linguistic and cultural backgrounds similar to those of the clients served. He also maintained that therapeutic and social service programs must be responsive to the socioeconomic pressures experienced by Mexicans and Chicanos.

Overall, common threads or themes ran through the papers presented. However, there were also diverse and conflicting perspectives reflecting the experiences and theoretical frameworks of the authors. With the exception of Atencio, none of the authors addressed the ideological foundations of the models they presented. However, Gallegos, Souflée, Romero, and Vazquez referred to issues or posed questions of an ideological nature. It is interesting to note that the six papers on models were conceptualized in mental health centers, within the framework of traditional mental health practice settings, or within the framework of existing social work theoretical constructs. That is to say, the genesis or initial point was not the "Chicano experience," ethos, or even ideology, but social work practice as it is or has been formulated by the majority or dominant society.

## Remaining Questions

Two themes appeared to be shared by the authors. All the presenters seemed to agree that despite progress made in the area of training and development of mental health services for Chicanos, the need of this population group is still great. Also, regardless of the labels used, they concurred in identifying culture and language as significant aspects in social work intervention with Chicanos.

Romero, Vazquez, and Saenz, the three practitioners actively involved in mental health practice within traditional mental health centers, proposed intervention approaches that emphasized advocacy and community action and focused on institutional or systemic change. However, the more academic authors oriented toward practice and research (Souflée, Gomez, and Silva) presented models focused primarily on intervention with clients and their immediate social or environmental context. Although they were not functioning within the constraints of such traditional settings as mental health centers, their approaches seemed to be defined within the boundaries of traditional social work intervention. All of them included language and culture as important variables to be considered. As indicated by Gallegos, the inclusion of the cultural variable as an important factor in social work education and practice may have been the most significant gain by Chicanos in the last decade.

Although the training of Chicano and Chicana social workers during the last decade has been significant (based on recent trends in enrollment, one could estimate that there are currently about 3,000 professional social workers who are Chicanos), the gain is inadequate in the light of the size of the client population and its socioeconomic plight. Furthermore, the gains are tenuous at best, given the decrease in enrollment of Chicanos in schools of social work and the elimination of mental health services as a result of federal cuts in funding.

The question raised by Gallegos, "To what end?" and posed by Atencio from a different perspective, "Can la Raza survive despite social services? Or can la Raza live without them?" should be restated within the context of our current historical situation. Should our emphasis in this decade, as in the last, be on services to Chicanos? Have social and mental health services empowered communities of Chicanos in the past? Have Chicano and Chicana social workers become a marginal middle-class buffer between the dominant majority and Chicanos? What ideological direction should guide the efforts of Chicano and Chicana social work educators and practitioners?

The papers presented at the workshop did not give conclusive answers to these searching questions, but they advanced the state of the art a few steps by helping us understand the progress made within the context of the present status of Chicanos and the potential positive and negative contributions social and mental health services can make. Above all, this collection has redirected our attention to the concept postulated by the French social theorists Jamous and Peloilla, that ideology conceived as part of a profession's domain gives identity and power to the profession.[2] Social and mental health services in the absence of a viable social reform movement are reduced to ameliorative or palliative efforts, as stated by Souflée at the workshop, and are incapable of changing the status of oppressed people.

## Notes and References

1. William Schwartz, "Between Client and System: The Mediating Function," in Robert W. Roberts and Helen Northen, eds., *Theories of Social Work with Groups* (New York: Columbia University Press, 1976); and Lawrence Shulman, "A Study of Practice Skills," *Social Work*, 23 (July 1978), pp. 274-280.

2. J. Jamous and B. Peloilla, "Changes in the French University Hospital System," in John A. Jackson, ed., *Professions and Professionalization*, Sociological Studies No. 3 (Cambridge, England: Cambridge University Press, 1970).

# Additional Papers

These papers were not presented at the "State of the Art" Workshop. However, they are included here because they deal with issues of concern to all Chicanos and expand the philosophical and strategic questions discussed.

# Ethnic Content in
# Social Work Education

*Eunice C. Garcia*

The issue of how to prepare social workers for practice in a pluralistic society came to the fore in the history of social work education at the same time that the civil rights movement was having its greatest impact in the United States. This article is an attempt to review the dialogue on the subject and to summarize epistemological assumptions in the literature. In the wake of this issue many questions were raised that have yet to be answered by individual schools of social work. For the profession at large, the issue and its attendant questions emerged and developed between 1964 and 1973.

Gordon wrote in 1964 that "in terms of crucial considerations of social structure intergroup relations in the United States proceed like a race horse galloping along with blinders. He doesn't know where he's been, he doesn't know where he is, and he doesn't know where he's going. But he's making progress."[1] That, in essence, was the milieu in which the Civil Rights Act of 1964 became law. The act was to outlaw racial discrimination and halt funds to federal projects that tolerated discrimination.

Although the Council on Social Work Education (CSWE) had had an accreditation standard regarding discriminatory policies since 1962, this civil rights legislation provided extra recruiting incentive to a profession suffering from a lack of trained practitioners. President Johnson provided two other boosters to social work: he articulated the need for more trained workers in social welfare and launched the War on Poverty. Social workers applauded all three moves without due consideration of the structural implications they carried for the profession. Thus, recruitment efforts undertaken by schools of social work as a result of CSWE's stance simply shifted their focus to the recruitment of minorities.[2] The literature shows no preparatory work regarding the special needs of such a new constituency in social work education—none, that is, beyond consideration of the immediate economic needs of schools and the recruits. It is no wonder, then, that the new minority students soon rose in collective frustration, for they found schools of social work to "function as institutions historically and culturally conditioned to promote Anglo-American attitudes, values, and behaviors."[3] Fact or not, that was their perspective, and as such it merited the attention of the council.

In 1969, CSWE established a Committee on Minority Groups, later to become the Commission on Minority Groups, to study the progress of compliance with the Civil Rights Act of 1964 and charged it to investigate the adequacy of financial assistance for students within the recruitment and retention process. The committee defined itself as chiefly concerned with the five major nonwhite groups represented in the United States (Mexican Americans, Puerto Ricans, blacks, Asian Americans, and American Indians) and soon served as a forum for the disgruntled new recruits. In 1970, it recommended the formation of task forces to deal with their concerns.[4] Each task force, representing a different racial or ethnic group, met with the aid of the council's Division on Minority Groups and ultimately produced reports that included recommendations for consideration by the council. In 1971 CSWE's House of Delegates passed a resolution that content related to minorities be integrated into social work curricula.[5] Exactly how that was to be done was left unresolved or was perhaps intended to be resolved by each individual school. A more detailed look at the various positions taken on the issue will follow a brief review of the literature.

## Pluralism and Practice

Preparation for practice in a pluralistic society is now mandated for social work education. As used here, pluralism refers to "a state in society in which members of diverse ethnic, racial, religious, or social groups maintain an autonomous participation in and development of their traditional culture or special interests within the confines of a common civilization."[6] Assuming that opposition to racial discrimination does not automatically mean support of pluralism, the author examined social work literature to determine attitudes toward pluralism.

A cursory review of the literature written by social work practitioners and educators during the 1960s revealed a growing preoccupation with service delivery to minority groups. Most of the articles of the period prior to 1965 dealt with pragmatic needs; there was no call for well-formulated theory regarding work with minorities. The *Encyclopedia of Social Work* summarized the profession's role in the area of race and welfare in the following manner:

> During the late 1940s and early 1950s, professional social work issues addressed race primarily as ethnic or cultural factors in practice relationships. In the late 1950s and early 1960s attention shifted to an emphasis on achieving the ideals of integration through the promulgation of nondiscriminatory agency policies. Such policies connoted omitting any consideration of race, color, creed, or ethnic origin in determining eligi-

bility for service or hiring staff. It became increasingly apparent that
the stance of "color blindness" accomplished little in opening access
to services . . . .[7]

The implication is that the concept of pluralism had not yet been
adopted; rather, the focus was on nondiscriminatory practice. A notable exception to this analysis was Berry's 1963 address to the
National Conference on Social Welfare, in which she advocated integration within social service delivery and stated that "an extension of
this, . . . is the right of clients to have service *according to their special
needs.*"[8] This was representative of a trend that Trattner later referred
to as a revival of social reform and an introduction to consumer
participation.[9]

Further examination of social work literature on race and welfare
revealed that in the late 1960s and early 1970s the focus was still
more on nondiscriminatory practices and less on the need for consideration of pluralism as a context within which social services
could begin to be individualized for the consumer. There were special
but scattered attempts to acquaint social workers with the nature and
implication of compensatory justice—that is, conscious discrimination in favor of minorities—and the various ethnic movements. This
provoked counterarguments, such as that of Teicher, who in 1972
argued in favor of nonminorities and against redistributive justice.[10]
There were other publications of interest: one tried to determine
whether there would be a black revolution; another described four
types of black protest and called for social workers to be aware of
the black power movement.[11] Aside from reports on the delibera-
tions taking place within CSWE's Committee on Minority Groups,
prior to 1972 little else was published concerning the preparation of
social workers for practice in a pluralistic society. The scarcity of
such material, however, does not mean that dialogue on the issue did
not exist.

By mid-1972, there were significant attempts within issues of
*Social Work* and the *Journal of Education for Social Work* to address
the needs of racial and ethnic minorities. *Social Work* dedicated its
entire May 1972 issue to "Ethnicity and Social Work," allowing
Turner's article on education for practice with minorities to explore
the recruitment and curriculum issues in social work education. By
differentiating between core content for all students and that needed
by students intending to work primarily with minority clients,
Turner spelled out the nature of the content needed to make curricula more relevant for training students for effective practice in an
"open" society. He argued that all students should be able to identify
and work to eliminate the vestiges of individual and institutional

racism within their agencies and "respond constructively and instrumentally to minority- or majority-group efforts that are intended to eliminate racism."[12] Turner also implied some students could be allowed to "specialize" in minority-majority problems through provisions for special content that included more in-depth knowledge about family, minority group, and individual culturally determined dynamics, as differentiated from those that tend to be a function of class status. He stressed the student's need for skills with which to facilitate coalitions whenever possible and aid the efforts of both minority and majority groups to gain social justice.

## Debate on Ethnic Content

At CSWE's 1973 annual meeting, Crompton presented a paper on the question of how to teach ethnic content.[13] He suggested that social work educators learn from the training program run by the Peace Corps for its volunteers. As early as 1968, he said, the Peace Corps had rejected the traditional information-transmission approach, because it was found that transmitting information on the history, politics, economics, arts, and peculiarities of a culture had resulted in training that was "little better than no training at all." This was further attributed to the "irrelevant" nature of the information provided by scholars, historians, and anthropologists, whose observer role differed so much from the participant role of the Peace Corps volunteer. Crompton suggested the development of process curricula in social work education through the utilization of the "Experiential Learning Model." This model used any culture different from the trainee's to sensitize the trainee to his or her own culture and to the differences in the way other people live.

Meanwhile, as the activities of CSWE's five task forces developed, a ripple effect was caused throughout individual schools of social work. Consequently, many educators were called on to write and speak on the issue of how to educate social work students for effective practice in a pluralistic society. Although little of the resulting material was ever published, a number of papers presented in workshops at schools in Texas and Louisiana became available for review and analysis. Most of the speakers took positions comparable to those articulated by the council's task force groups. No one was as explicit in expressing concern about the abundance of discussion but lack of sufficient action as Sanchez, who urged the following:

> We should spend less time on identifying and discussing ethnic curriculum content and materials, and more energy on incorporating the ethnic content and materials we now have. . . . The process of incorporating ethnic curriculum content generates the process of further development and refinement of ethnic curriculum content. For knowledge begins with

practice, and theoretical knowledge which is acquired through practice must return to practice.[14]

The material produced during this time documents the efforts of specific schools to relate to minority issues and alludes to the main concerns faced by the social work profession within the period of 1964 to 1973.[15] In essence, the shortage of trained social workers led to the recruitment of minority group members, and concern for effective service delivery led in turn to the consideration of how to prepare social work students for effective practice with minorities. The reports of the CSWE task forces, which appeared around this time, represented a concerted effort to establish guidelines for recruitment and educational relevancy for minorities within social work education.[16] Their divergent content offers key material regarding the dialogue on the issue of how to educate students for effective practice in a pluralistic society.

## Task Force Efforts

Of the five CSWE task forces, one of the most vocal groups demanding greater recruitment of students and faculty, community participation, and relevance in curricula was the Puerto Rican Task Force. Its initial presentation was no less than a set of demands calling for redistributive education, that is, for a focus on the recruitment of Puerto Ricans in regions with Puerto Rican populations, the replacement of regular faculty vacancies with Puerto Rican faculty, and the development of curriculum and fieldwork focus on the theory and practice skills needed for service delivery in the Puerto Rican community on the mainland as well as on the island of Puerto Rico. This task force called for differentiating needs in the Puerto Rican community from those of the black community.

Initially the American Indian Task Force was not involved in the articulation of needs at the curriculum level. It focused on greater efforts for the recruitment of American Indians into schools of social work. The Asian American and the Mexican American Task Forces were very similar in that they called for proportionate representation among students and faculty, but they also focused on the need for more relevant curricula. The Black Task Force was very different from the other four; it focused on recommendations concerning curricula. The head start it got in 1969 through sponsorship of black social work organizations placed it at a great advantage over the other groups, whose leadership was also less influential in the profession. Nevertheless, by 1973, all but the American Indian and Asian American Task Forces had gone beyond the position of citing material on historical background and institutional racism as the content needed within social work curricula. By the end of the following year, the five task forces had enumerated and defended a wide range of positions, a sampling of which appears below:

☐ All social work students need theory (ethnic content) and skills for effective practice with given minority groups.

☐ Only students of a given minority group should be trained to work with such a group; they know their culture in a way no one else can grasp it.

☐ Sensitization to a specific culture is a prerequisite for all nonminority students and faculty if historical and cultural content is to be taught at all.

☐ It is not safe to assume that all minority students are culturally aware; they, too, must be sensitized.

☐ Social work students must know the historical roots of minority groups with whom they expect to work. They must also understand institutional racism. These two areas of knowledge are prerequisites for effective practice.

☐ The way to train students for practice in a pluralistic society is to place them in practicum settings within the ghetto (or *barrio*\*) that correspond with pivotal programs of that specific community system.

☐ The way to provide adequate education for practice in a pluralistic society is to place students in a practicum with instruction from that particular community, for example, from *barrio* professors—social work instructors indigenous to a community, who do not have formal credentials but are experts on the community.

☐ Social work students should be required to take "ethnic courses," that is, courses about ethnic or racial minorities taught by minority faculty.

☐ Ethnic content must be integrated into behavioral and practice courses.

☐ Ethnic content must be developed within research courses.

☐ Ethnic content is already available in ethnic studies within larger university settings. Therefore, enrollment in such courses could be required or be optional.

☐ Ethnic content is available in case study material developed by each individual student working with minority clientele; the instructor's role is to conceptualize the material within more general theory.[17]

---

\*The translation of this and other Spanish words can be found in the glossary at the end of this book.

These are but twelve of many more positions that could be listed. The dialogue had several unexpected outcomes. Ultimately, only the blacks and Mexican Americans were to share similar thoughts on needed content.[18] The Asian Americans wrote of their isolated experience and their neglected situation, while the Puerto Ricans emerged as separatists, defending their orientation in view of a problem they claimed as theirs, the "lack of identity" among younger Puerto Ricans.[19] CSWE planned to sponsor a developmental experience in social work education systematically and comprehensively for the five constituencies. However, in 1973, it turned its attention to a "new" group — women.

Currently, CSWE's official position reflecting its "resolution" of the issue of how to prepare students for practice in a pluralistic society is that ethnic content should be integrated into social work curricula. However, the resolution's lack of epistemological clarity, accompanied by the task forces' failure to clarify their respective epistemological orientations, reinforces the vagueness of the official mandate. The issue is now in the hands of each individual school of social work. Moreover, how it is handled may be up to the discretion of faculty committees or to that of each faculty member of the individual school. In other words, the issue of how to prepare social work students for effective practice in a pluralistic society is still unresolved for social work education at large. The council's resolution was left at a level of abstract speculation, and its lack of clarity is contrary to pragmatic educational goals.

## Implications for Mexican Americans

In all fairness, given the numerous positions reflected by the minority task forces, perhaps the council's mandate was as precise as it could have been. The process involving these key minority constituencies did reinforce and have an impact on efforts directed at recruitment of minority faculty and students and the integration of ethnic content. The council's task forces also initiated a process of collaboration among members of each of these groups. Most important, the process revealed that although there were some common concerns, each group could most comfortably and competently state its own interests and positions. More than a decade has passed since CSWE's "resolution" of this issue. No doubt it is time to rekindle an interest in it by calling for a more precise stance on goals and methods by which to train social workers for effective practice with Mexican Americans.

An examination of various publications may serve to review briefly the subsequent development of ideas regarding services to Mexican Americans and relevant teaching approaches. In an article appearing in

1975, Gibson reflected on mental health services for Mexican Americans, commenting that

> for many people, particularly for Chicanos in the barrio, services remain inadequate, incompatible, and incongruent linguistically and culturally, and often inaccessible psychologically, and even at times geographically. Granted that mental health practitioners are modifying their service delivery styles (some with considerable success), searching for effective ways to serve the people in the barrios. . . .[20]

Gibson advocated a bilingual-bicultural approach and added, "Keeping in mind that Chicanos are bicultural and bilingual individuals, all mental health personnel should develop bilingual skills and sensitivity to the culture if they are committed to serve the barrio." She also suggested the exchange of cultural knowledge for professional skill. Similar concern for Mexican Americans as underserved clients was echoed during the Texas-New Mexico symposium on the delivery of mental health services to Mexican Americans.[21]

In addition, the Chicano Training Center of Houston, Texas, launched an effort to develop curriculum models for the infusion of content related to Mexican Americans. The impetus was attributed to the need for Mexican Americans to continue the process of developing such content. Members of white ethnic groups, it was predicted, would dilute the focus that until then had been aided by the political environment of the late 1960s.[22] The teaching models developed sought to comply with the council's mandate for infusion of ethnic content, and all three models linked and emphasized the need for theoretical and experiential content for all students.

To sum up, more than a decade after the "resolution" of this issue, content related to Mexican Americans remains to be integrated into all social work curricula. As previously mentioned, there also remains considerable concern about the adequacy of services provided to Mexican American clients. Moreover, although more Mexican Americans are now in the educational system and potentially available for recruitment into social work, the current retrenchment in funds for training and service projects and the increase in the numbers of Mexican Americans and Hispanics from Latin America among the population may soon erode any real headway that may have been achieved by earlier recruitment efforts. These realities have a direct bearing on how Mexican Americans must now shape a role in the new era of social services.

## Issues for Resolution

These new realities pose some questions. For instance, given a reduction of funds to recruit and support Mexican American trainees, should we now support training all students for effective work with Mexican

Americans? Should we continue to create alternative training models for use by faculty charged with the infusion of content related to Mexican Americans? Should we even seek consensus and take an official stance regarding any of these issues?

This last question raises a much more fundamental issue. Intracultural diversity and biculturalism are not only concepts, they are realities that shape our behavior at the personal and professional level. Together, they trigger a phenomenon that we warmly embrace when we say *Cada cabeza es un mundo*. Name all possible areas where Mexican American educators or practitioners may have elected to invest their energy, and you are sure to find some of us there. The spectrum, therefore, is both beautiful and complex. How can we ever expect to agree on all these issues that have an impact on the role we, in a collective sense, may need to address? Again, should we even try? This writer believes that total group deliberation and consensus are unrealistic and unnecessary. Nevertheless, it is imperative that we have additional dialogue and consolidation of goals and approaches. For example, if we are indeed satisfied with the movement toward the experiential-theoretical approach in teaching because it is most relevant to current social work curricula, then we should articulate this preference and proceed to refine our expectations of such an approach in terms of competence. We should concentrate on developing more educational tools for use by all people involved in teaching about Mexican Americans. This does not mean that we must become evangelical about an approach. However, there is a need to share more of our thoughts and approaches (and responsibility) with the rest of our colleagues in order to collaborate more systematically in the development of the practice and teaching models we so desperately need. In other words, individualism and its consequent competitiveness have a time and place but should not preclude our actively supporting each other's efforts and, whenever possible, assisting each other in testing new ideas and models. For instance, why should it take one of us five years to try an approach with different class groups, when several of us could do the same with more groups in less time? Although this may not seem too grave an issue to Mexican Americans who work alongside other Mexican Americans, there are others who are isolated in their organizations and who may need this interchange of ideas and active collaboration with their peers.

Some of the educational issues that we must now address include the following:

1. What cross-cultural helping competencies should we require of all entry-level practitioners?

2. What ethnic-specific knowledge and culturally relevant methodologies can we include in undergraduate programs and in graduate programs?

3. What new content needs to be developed regarding the experience of Mexican Americans and the analysis of new practice models for use with Mexican American clients?

4. What new teaching approaches or units need to be developed for use in classroom teaching? In field teaching?

5. Where and how can we join other ethnic groups in their efforts to make social work more responsive to the needs of minorities?

We have come a long way in less than twenty years, since the height of the civil rights movement. Because the journey has really just begun, we must not let the current economic and political crisis halt this initial impetus. Perhaps we can now consider another alternative. Although retrenchment of resources may prohibit expansion, we must resolve to use this period to analyze what has been accomplished and develop tools to assure quality in our contributions in social work. A Dios orando y con el mazo dando!

## Notes and References

1. Milton Gordon, *Assimilation in American Life: The Role of Race, Religion and National Origins* (New York: Oxford University Press, 1964), p. 9.

2. Katherine Kendall, "Issues and Problems in Social Work Education," *Social Work Education Reporter*, 14 (March 1966), pp. 34-36.

3. Rosina Becerra, *Chicanos: A Student Report on Social Work Education* (San Diego, Calif.: Satellite Office Service, 1971), p. 15.

4. James R. Dumpson, "Special Committee on Minority Groups," *Social Work Education Reporter*, 18 (March 1970), pp. 28-30 and 66-67.

5. This spearheaded activity that resulted in the establishment of CSWE's anti-discrimination standard 1234A. See *Manual of Accrediting Standards for Graduate and Professional Schools of Social Work* (New York: Council on Social Work Education, April 1971).

6. *Webster's New Collegiate Dictionary* (3d ed.; Springfield, Mass.: G. & C. Merriam Co., 1975), p. 885.

7. James O.F. Hackshaw, "Race and Welfare," *Encyclopedia of Social Work*, Vol. 2 (rev. ed.; Washington, D.C.: National Association of Social Workers, 1973), p. 1065.

8. Margaret Berry, "Civil Rights and Social Welfare," *Social Welfare Forum, 1963* (New York: Columbia University Press, 1963), p. 85.

9. Walter I. Trattner, *From Poor Law to Welfare State: A History of Social Welfare in America* (New York: Free Press, 1974), p. 263.

10. Morton Teicher, "Reverse Discrimination," *Social Work*, 17 (November 1972), pp. 3-4.

11. See Hylan Lewis, "Race, the Polity, and the Professions," *Journal of Education for Social Work*, 5 (Fall 1969), pp. 19-30; and Murray Gruber, "Four Types of Black Protest: A Study," *Social Work*, 18 (January 1973), pp. 42-51.

12. John B. Turner, "Education for Practice with Minorities," *Social Work*, 17 (May 1972), p. 115.

13. See Don W. Crompton, "Minority Content in Social Work Education — Promise or Pitfall?" *Journal of Education for Social Work*, 10 (Winter 1974), pp. 9-18.

14. Rodolfo B. Sanchez, "A Chicano Perspective on Social Work Curriculum Development," p. 2. Paper presented at the workshop on "The Relevancy of Black and Chicano Content: Rationale, Rhyme and Reason," Houston, Tex., April 13 and 14, 1972.

15. More specific information concerning this material is available on request from the author.

16. See Magdalena Miranda, ed., *Puerto Rican Task Force Report*, Angel P. Compos, ed., *Puerto Rican Curriculum Development Workshop: A Report*, John E. Mackey, ed., *American Indian Task Force Report*, Kenji Murase, ed., *Asian American Task Force Report: Problems and Issues in Social Work Education*, Juliette Ruiz, ed., *Chicano Task Force Report*, and Richard Lodge, ed., *Black Perspectives in Social Work Education: Issues Related to Curriculum, Faculty and Students* (New York: Council on Social Work Education, 1973, 1974, 1973, 1973, 1973, and 1974, respectively).

17. Ibid.

18. Raul DeAnda and Vernon Lockett, "Introducing Black and Chicano Content into a Social Work Curriculum: A Recommendation," *Social Work Education Reporter*, 20 (October 1972), pp. 28-31.

19. Murase, op. cit.; and Miranda, op. cit.

20. Guadalupe Gibson, "Training Aspects in Working with Chicanos," *Mano A Mano*, 4 (August 1975), pp. 1-4.

21. Federico Souflée, Jr. and George Valdez, eds., *Proceedings of the Texas-New Mexico Symposium on the Delivery of Mental Health Services to Mexican-Americans* (Houston, Tex.: Chicano Training Center, 1978).

22. Norma Benavides and Federico Souflée, Jr., eds., *A Course Syllabi Compendium* (Houston, Tex.: Chicano Training Center, 1978), pp. vi-vii.

# La Mortificación:
# An Interactional View

*Alvin O. Korte*

*Yo tengo mortificaciónes; tu tienes mortificaciónes; todos tenemos mortificaciónes!*\* We all have minor and major troubles that beset us. *La mortificación* is a term used by middle- and older-generation Spanish-speaking people to refer to mortification, or troubles that disturb their well-being and peace of mind.[1]

Chicano and Chicana social workers have for some time been concerned with developing perspectives and understanding concerning the mental health of Chicanos. A study of the various terms that relate to well-being in the lexicon of Chicanos can aid the mental health practitioner in understanding the perceptions of clients who are Chicanos. This article will elaborate on one concept, that of *mortificación*. However, the model of examination can be used to clarify other terms relating to well-being.

Denzin has argued that in researching the development of concepts, the investigator must first enter the field and learn the specific meanings attached to the processes represented by the concepts. This "permits the researcher to discover what is unique about each empirical instance of the concept while he uncovers what it displays in common, across many different settings. Such a conception forces (in fact allows) the sociologist to pursue the interactionist view of reality to the empirical extreme."[2] As an interactionist, Denzin also argues that concepts must ultimately be located and described in their interactional context. *Mortificación* will be explored as a concept through an analysis of its historical roots and its interactional attributes. Further, the relationship of the term to the Chicano perspectives of *plática*, *vergüenza*, and *respeto* will also be examined.

In various social strata and cultures, people experience vexations and being tormented by individuals whose behavior they would like to influence. These vexing interactions have many elements in common. Therefore, the present analysis will show the concept of *mortificación* as universal in its applicability.

## Definitions and Etymology

Perhaps the earliest references to *mortificación* can be found in *El Libro de San Cipriano*, a medieval treatise on the invocation of spells, pacts,

---

\*The translation of these and other Spanish words can be found in the glossary at the end of this book.

incantations, and exorcisms, written around 1000 A.D. by Sufurino.³ In chapter thirteen, Sufurino provides a procedure to determine if a person is suffering from natural sickness or is *mortificado* ("tormented") by an evil spirit. This exorcism calls on Archangel Michael for help in enchaining and humiliating this particular vexing demon.

This linking of *mortificación* with a malevolent spirit is also commonly heard among Spanish-speaking people in northern New Mexico. Thus, when an adult son has been drinking too much, his parents may identify his drinking as a *maleficio* ("evil") and their torment by it as their particular *mortificación*.

There are several definitions of *mortificación*: (1) mortification of the body by hardships and macerations, (2) gangrene, and (3) vexation or trouble. Definitions of the term *mortificar* are even more revealing and direct in their implications: (1) to mortify; to destroy vital qualities, (2) to subdue inordinate passions, (3) to afflict, disgust, or vex, and (4) to practice religious severities; to conquer one's passions.⁴

In addition, the *New Catholic Encyclopedia* defines mortification as

the deliberate restraining that one places on natural impulses in order to make them increasingly subject to sanctification through obedience to reason illuminated by faith. Jesus Christ required such renunciation of anyone who wished to come after him (Lk. 9:29). And so mortification or what St. Paul calls the crucifixion of the flesh with its vices and concupiscences (Gal. 5:24), has become a distinguishing mark of those who are Christ's.⁵

In this conception, mortification is seen as necessary for salvation because human beings are strongly inclined to evil by the threefold concupiscence of the world, the flesh, and the devil, which will lead to grievous sin if not restrained. Finally, those who seek to advance themselves in Christian perfection must mortify themselves more than ordinary believers do because "Christ made the bearing of a cross the price of being his close followers."⁶

Another historical and etymological aspect of mortification is its relationship to death, which is traceable from the Greek root word *thnetos*, meaning "subject or liable to death; mortal." In Rom. 6:12, the body is called "mortal," not simply because it is subject to death, but because it is the medium in and through which death carries on its activity. Similarly, mortify, from *thanatoo*, "to put to death" (from *thanatos*, "death," akin to *thnetos*, "mortal") is translated as "mortify" in Rom. 8:13, or to put to death "the deeds of the body."⁷ A religious order in northern New Mexico, the Brothers of Light, or *Los Penitentes*, were known to *mortificar el cuerpo* by special penances such as flagellations with whips made of cactus thorns and long marches on their knees during Holy Week.

In an etymological tracing of the *mr* root or consonants for a study of the significance of the nightmare, Jones argues that many *mr* root words signify sadistic and brutal action, as in to pound (a mortar), grind, crush, injure, bite, beat, gall, and oppress.[8] The Spanish term for nightmare is *pesadilla*, which can also refer to a difficult problem typically accompanied by strong feelings of anxiety, grief, or emotional oppression.

One aspect of the *mr* root means "to die; to be ruined." Another root, namely "mortal" or "mortify," as in the Latin, also means "to vex another." Later in this discussion the question of vexing another through *mortificación*, of causing the person to want to die, as in the Spanish expression *Pasé tantas vergüenzas y mortificaciónes que me quise morir* ("I felt so ashamed and humiliated I wanted to die"), will be developed further. A combination of *m* and *l* finds such words in Spanish as *mal*, meaning "evil." This root term of *mal* occurs in a variety of related words. *Maldición*, literally, "a curse," could also refer to the person cursed (*un maldicido*) as well as to being saddled with an unending, unendurable problem.

## Loss of the Self

The relationship between *mortificación* and malevolence is of interest in that it refers to the interaction between a person being vexed and the person causing the difficulties. A typical example is a parental complaint, *La borrachera de mi hijo es pura mortificación* ("My son's drinking is pure mortification"). Another example is the chagrin an elderly person might experience concerning a daughter newly released from a state hospital. This mother might remark, *Esta muchacha es una mortificación. Parece que nos pucieron un maleficio* ("This girl is a mortification. It seems as though we have been cursed"). Considered from a social interactionist perspective, a variety of *mortificaciónes*, such as a husband who is drinking too much, a delinquent son, or an adult daughter who is having difficulties with her husband, are all subject to the same analysis.

According to Lewis, mortification and chagrin belong to several variants of the "shame family" of feeling states. Originally, chagrin came from the French, where the word meaning "rough and granular skin employed to rub, polish or file, becomes by metaphor, the expression for gnawing trouble."[9] Now, says Lewis, the word means "that which worries or frets the mind; fretting trouble, care, anxiety, melancholia." The term "chagrin" adds an additional dimension to the varieties of shame, emphasizing the hostility accompanying shame and its "mental disquietude." Schneider also correlates shame and mortification and notes that the connections are many sided. Being exposed, which causes embarrassment or shame, leads to the feeling of wanting to die.[10] Paraphrasing Lewis, Schneider speaks of the feeling of dying in shame as an experience of the momentary loss of the self.

Common to all *mortificaciónes* is a change in self-esteem and self-image for the vexed person, the onset of profound embarrassment, and, in some cases, the freezing of action on the part of the vexed individual. The wish to die and the freezing of action implies also the "death" of the self that characterizes these particular types of situations.[11] In order to develop this thesis further, we must give consideration to the common everyday values related to saving face, which are *plática*, *respeto*, and *confianza*. It is the violation of these values that causes humiliation, *vergüenza* ("shame"), and, hence, devaluations of the self.

## Saving Face

In face-to-face interactions, one person meeting another wonders if his or her presentation of self will be respected and upheld. Goffman describes "face" as the positive social valuations a person claims for himself or herself by the "line" or tack others assume he or she has taken during a particular interaction.[12]

In presenting the self to others, the Spanish-speaking person assesses a variety of significant considerations in the interaction. How much should he or she reveal? How will the "contents" (or, in Goffman's terminology, the line) be evaluated and upheld?

As a value manifested in social interaction, *respeto* ("respect") means a quality of self presented in all interpersonal relations. *Respeto*, as Lauria points out, means proper attention to the requisites of the ceremonial order of behavior and of the moral aspects of human activities. *Respeto* involves proper demeanor. Lauria suggests that *un hombre de respeto* is "a proper 'interactant,' committed to, and capable of, maintaining another man's image of himself."[13] He is said to be *un hombre de consideración*—a man who has consideration for the self-image of others—but such an individual might more correctly be termed *una persona de respeto* (or *consideración*) because *respeto* involves proper demeanor for both sexes.

Proper attention to the line of another means that the interacting other will be allowed to save or maintain the proper face. If face is maintained, the individual is said to have *consideración* or *respeto* for the presentation of the other's self. Such a *persona de consideración* can be said to be someone in whom one can have *confianza* ("trust"), for he or she maintains and protects one's valued self-image. These expectations are the routine grounds of everyday social interactions. What highlights the existence of these norms for interaction is their violation, as when an individual knowingly disregards these taken-for-granted expectations in interactions.

Several other considerations are important. Among Chicanos *plática* ("warm, friendly conversation") is considered a viable means of understanding the "otherness" of the person with whom one is interacting. *Plática* as a value manifests itself in such statements as *Platicando se entienden las cosas* ("By conversing, people can understand each other's situation"). *Plática* understood in this sense may mean that true *confianza* can be built into a relationship. Santistevan has it that *estar de acuerdo* ("to be in accord") may mean that two interactants understand each other's position and have confidence that their face will not be destroyed in future interactions.[14] As such, both interactants can now maintain poise and develop *confianza* in each other.

An elderly man on welfare invited me into his house with the following statements: *Vamos a platicar. Platicando se entienden las cosas.* In effect, the invitation to share aspects of himself meant that he wanted me to understand his situation as well as that of his family. By doing so he assumed that I would represent him fairly and honestly with those who administered the welfare program. Failure to do so on my part would mean a normative violation causing him *vergüenza.* It would also mean that I had become a shameless person, a *sin vergüenza*, and a *descarado* (literally, "a person without face"), because I would be unable to maintain and preserve his face to others.

*Plática*, then, serves as a means by which two interactants present to each other various facets of their organized and valued selves. To violate norms related to this perspective is to become a heartless person. Goffman has it "that in the dominant culture a person who can witness another's humiliation and unfeelingly retain a cool countenance himself is said to be 'heartless.' He who can unfeelingly participate in his own defacement is thought to be 'shameless.' "[15] Northern New Mexico culture brands these interactants as *descarados.*

In Laing's view, a growing dissatisfaction exists with any theory or study of the individual that isolates the person from his or her social context.[16] One cannot give an account of someone without giving an account of his or her relations with others. Each person is always acting upon others and being acted upon by them. Laing points out that in complementarity the other fulfills or completes the self. One person may complement another in many different senses. All "identities" require another, or some other person in whom identity is actualized.

In everyday terms, to be *de acuerdo con otro* means that interactants have negotiated an accord. This accord has to do with meanings that are shared and will motivate future actions as well as provide the ground on which the closer relationship of *confianza* may be built and may begin to grow and, perhaps, eventually flourish.

## Aspects of Humiliation

Interaction is fraught with uncertainties. Accord may not be reached; identity claims may be made that are not met with deference and respect; *confianza* may not develop. Worse yet, in interactions that cause one of the participants to feel humiliated, such as in those encounters being called *mortificaciónes*, profound embarrassment and a desire to retreat quickly from the situation may ensue. What is it about the penetrability of the self by others that allows the self to be wounded and so humiliated in those forms of interaction termed *mortificaciónes?* A partial answer can be found in the work of Nuttin, who believes that the sense of shame is connected with one of the most characteristic features of psychological life, the combination of privacy and penetrability in human life.[17] On the other hand, psychological life is not purely interior and cannot be considered impenetrable by others. This penetrability of the private self is what may cause shame, as in the exposure of this interiority, which Nuttin calls "the functional conditions for the origin of shame."

Humiliating experiences, according to Lynd, threaten the very basis for the presentation of the self to others. One's core of identity is endangered and in effect destroyed. As Lynd explains,

> The characteristics that have been suggested as central in experiences of shame—the sudden exposure of unanticipated incongruity, the seemingly trivial incident that arouses overwhelming and almost unbearable painful emotion, the threat to the core of identity, the loss of trust in expectations of oneself, of other persons, of one's society, and a reluctantly recognized question of meaning in the world—all these things combine to make experiences of shame almost impossible to communicate.[18]

Gross and Stone point out that situations causing embarrassment also incapacitate people in terms of role performance.[19] Embarrassing situations leave the individual exposed and incapable of continuing to perform the role at hand. The person may break into tears, take flight, or, in extreme situations, commit suicide—not to save face, but because face has been destroyed beyond repair.

Natanson, in his phenomenological analysis of role performance, differentiates various aspects of social role as "the complex of societally formed requirements for understanding and performing patterned action in social roles." He defines role-taking as "the dynamics for effecting and carrying out such roles in actual practice," and, relevant to this analysis, role-action as "the intentional dimension underlying role-taking."[20]

Natanson not only considers the intentionality of role-taking as occurring prior to role-action, but he also outlines five assumptions that underlie role-action. These are the following:

☐ *Openness.* There is a "role to be taken." The social space is open for action, and the actor has the power to take the role.

☐ *Repeatability.* The role-taker has played the role before and may reassume prior roles.

☐ *Familiarity.* The role-taker knows what to do in the role. It is regainable in familiar form.

☐ *Recognition.* The role-taker puts a personal stamp on the role. The actor's idiosyncratic aspect is merged with the role-taking.

☐ *Release.* The role is completed. The social action has a discernible end.

These conditions allow the role taker to assume roles within a given segment of intervals available for role-taking.[21]

Natanson's five essential assumptions underlying role-action and role-taking are used in his analysis of the effects of alienation on the ability to mobilize action. The abstract capacity involved in each of the elements of role-action, as well as in their synthetic operation, is deformed in experiences of alienation. The role-taker who attempts to reconstruct social reality or a role from a purely abstract or noetic dimension is unable to reconstruct the steps needed in order to act. The taken-for-granted cultural values that prescribe the behavior between interactants are no longer in effect in interactions termed *mortificaci-ónes*. The role-taker or person mortified is in an interactive situation in which the familiar grounds for interaction are frustrated, altered, or destroyed. For Chicanos, elements of *respeto* and *vergüenza* that guide interaction no longer seem to hold true. *Plática* becomes impossible. Small wonder that the mortified person feels caught in an unfamiliar or threatening situation from which he or she wishes to flee.

## Inability to Act

Goffman and Gross and Stone have pointed to people's inability to implement role functions in social situations that cause embarrassment.[22] Because mortification has much in common with the family of shaming experiences, some content from Goffman is apropos. For Goffman, the completely flustered or embarrassed individual is

> one who cannot for the time being mobilize his muscular and intellectual resources for the task at hand, although he would like to; he cannot volunteer a response to those around him that will allow them to sustain

the conversation smoothly. He and his flustered actions block the line of activity the others have been pursuing. He is present with them, but he is not in play.[23]

Because of this, the vexed person is unable to maintain his or her poise in interactions in which vexing, obnoxious, haranguing, and often-times brutal physical exchanges occur. For example, a vexed person who is assuming the role of father or mother toward an alcoholic son or a mentally ill daughter may find the social components available for action essentially deformed. That is, the familiar and taken-for-granted assumptions of the parental role are no longer in effect. The vexed individual who must mobilize action cannot assume the parental role because the assumptions underlying role-action and role-taking identi-fied by Natanson no longer apply. He or she tries to maintain poise and identity as a parent toward someone whose identity and behavior have essentially become unknown. Mental anguish or *mortificación* ensues.

As Goffman has noted, embarrassment occurs when the flustered individual is considered to exhibit weakness, inferiority, low status, moral guilt, defeat, and other unenviable attributes.[24] In the lexicon of Chicanos, one's perceived failure as a parent translates even more clearly into *vergüenza*, which is not necessarily a private affair that affects only the individual who experiences it. Rather, it is faced before family members, significant others, and the community as well. Vexed parents, for example, may feel that they are no longer *respetados* ("respected"), that their *consejos* ("wise counsel") are not accepted, and, finally, that they are unable to perform their role.

Becker argues that the self is largely a locus of word possibilities. We become uncomfortable in strange groups and subcultures largely because we cannot frame an easy verbal transition to sustain action. Self-esteem is threatened because "not only do words enable us to protect ourselves by confidently manipulating the interpersonal situa-tion; also, by verbally setting the tone for action by proper ritual for-mulas, we permit complementary action by our interlocutor."[25]

Becker further maintains that words not only "sustain us by outlin-ing a context of action in which we can be meaningfully motivated," they also, in a sense, "create" us, "by infusing our action with mean-ing." He goes on to say that "as we act meaningfully we exercise our powers and create our identity."[26] Thus, if *mortificación* leads to an inability to act, a freezing of action, identity presentation becomes impossible. We have no words to describe our chagrin and humiliation. Small wonder the importance of the statement *Pasé tantas vergüenzas y mortificaciónes que me quise morir.* The vocabulary of victimization is indicative of a self unable to create an identity. *Mortificación* thus becomes a death of the self.

In summary, *mortificación* is only one term in the everyday dictionary of emotions of Chicanos. An elderly person interviewed by me observed that *La paciencia retira la mortificación* ("Patience alleviates mortification"). This indicates that Chicanos may have practical, everyday strategies for dealing with *mortificaciónes*. However, social scientists and mental health practitioners have not paid much attention to the study of coping mechanisms among Chicanos. Ramos showed how Chicanos use *movidas*, a common sense approach, in coping with and managing their daily lives.[27] He points out that we should use the troubles people create for each other in their day-to-day existence for the study of coping and managing strategies. Not only can we learn how Chicanos symbolize their social reality but also how they understand, cope, and manage everyday problem situations.

## Notes and References

1. Arthur Rubel, "Concepts of Disease in Mexican-American Culture," *American Anthropologist*, 62 (October 1960), pp. 795-814.

2. Norman Denzin, "The Methodologies of Symbolic Interaction: A Critical Review of Research Techniques," in Gregory P. Stone and Harvey A. Farberman, eds., *Social Psychology Through Symbolic Interaction* (Waltham, Mass.: Xerox College Publishing, 1970), pp. 455-456.

3. Jonas Sufurino, *El Libro de San Cipriano: Libro Completo e Verdadera Magia o Sea Tesoro del Hechicero* (Mexico, Distrito Federal: Biblioteca Ciencias Ocultas, undated).

4. *New Revised Velásquez Spanish and English Dictionary* (Chicago: Follett Publishing Co., 1967), p. 467.

5. *New Catholic Encyclopedia* (New York: McGraw-Hill Book Co., 1967), p. 1153.

6. Ibid.

7. W.E. Vine, *An Expository Dictionary of New Testament Words* (Old Tappum, N.J.: Fleming H. Revell Co., 1966), pp. 84-85.

8. Ernest Jones, *On the Nightmare* (New York: Grove Press, 1951), pp. 332-333.

9. Helen B. Lewis, *Shame and Guilt in Neurosis* (New York: International Universities Press, 1971), p. 73.

10. Carl D. Schneider, *Shame, Exposure and Privacy* (Boston: Beacon Press, 1979), pp. 78-79.

11. Some recent doctoral dissertations mention the *mortificaciónes* of elderly Chicanos but do not explore situational aspects of these phenomena in detail. However, Rubel mentions the distraught "Mrs. Benitez," who feared beatings from her husband and altercations with her son-in-law that caused her many *mortificaciónes*. "Mrs. Benitez" described her situation as living *asustada*, meaning that a part of her self, the *espíritu*, is caused to leave her body. A person who suffers long, continuous periods of languor, listlessness, and a lack of appetite is presumed to be *asustado(a)*.

Rubel indicates that various forms of the verb *mortificar* are often used by Chicanos to describe a traumatic personal reaction to upsetting situations. The *asustado* condition, as used as an everyday depiction by Chicanos, could be thought to fit into the fabric of "the loss of self" as delineated in the present discussion. See op. cit. Further information on dissertations referring to *mortificación* is available from the author.

12. Erving Goffman, "On Face Work," in Goffman, *Interaction Ritual* (New York: Doubleday & Co., 1967), pp. 10-11.

13. Anthony Lauria, Jr., "Respeto, Relajo and Interpersonal Relations in Puerto Rico," *Anthropological Quarterly,* 37 (April 1964), pp. 54-55.

14. Interview with Pablo Santistevan, Professor, Department of Social Work, New Mexico Highlands University, Las Vegas, N.M., September 27, 1979.

15. Goffman, op. cit., pp. 10-11.

16. R.D. Laing, *Self and Others* (New York: Penguin Books, 1969), p. 82.

17. Josef Nuttin, "Intimacy and Shame in the Dynamic Structure of Personality," in Martin L. Reymert, ed., *Feelings and Emotions: The Mooseheart Symposium* (New York: McGraw-Hill Book Co., 1950), pp. 344-345.

18. Helen M. Lynd, *On Shame and the Search for Identity* (New York: Harcourt, Brace & World, 1958), p. 64.

19. Edward Gross and Gregory P. Stone, "Embarrassment and the Analysis of Role Requirements," in Stone and Farberman, eds., *Social Psychology Through Symbolic Interaction*, p. 190.

20. Maurice Natanson, "Alienation and Social Role," in Natanson, *Phenomenology, Role and Reason: Essays on the Coherence and Deformation of Social Reality* (Springfield, Ill.: Charles C Thomas, Publisher, 1974), p. 177.

21. Ibid., pp. 182-185.

22. Erving Goffman, "Embarrassment and Social Organizations," in James Henslin, ed., *Down to Earth Sociology* (New York: Free Press, 1972), pp. 72-82; and Gross and Stone, op. cit.

23. Goffman, "Embarrassment and Social Organizations," p. 75.

24. Ibid., p. 76.

25. Ernest Becker, "The Self as a Locus of Linguistic Causality," in Dennis Brisset and Charles Edgley, eds., *Life as Theatre: A Dramaturgical Source Book* (Chicago: Aldine Publishing Co., 1975), p. 59.

26. Ibid., p. 62.

27. Reyes Ramos, "Movidas: The Methodological and Theoretical Relevance of Interactional Strategies," in Norman Denzin, ed., *Studies in Symbolic Interaction*, Vol. 2 (Greenwich, Conn.: Jal Press, 1979), p. 160.

# Recruiting Minorities: An Implementation Analysis

*Norma Benavides*

The relationship between academic programs and the field of social work practice has been an area of major debate. The issues of the nature of curriculum and the length of time required for the completion of the curriculum at different academic levels have received equal attention. These issues have particular relevance for minority professionals and students.

Although the period of the 1960s was characterized by a "swell of discontent" among students about the irrelevance of casework, this attitude was especially prevalent among those who were minority group members.[1] Of major importance to minority communities was the inaccessibility of professional training because of the strict admission standards of graduate schools of social work. For those minority students who were fortunate enough to gain entrance to a school, the irrelevance of the educational system to the needs of individuals in their communities became a primary concern. During this period, social work education came under "strong, sometimes violent, attack."[2] Because of the persistence of pressure regarding these issues, schools began to respond.

In the years since, many schools of social work have initiated special programs to increase their minority enrollment, and the Council on Social Work Education (CSWE) has been active in the enrollment effort.[3] Most of these programs have been government funded. Under the auspices of the U.S. Department of Health, Education, and Welfare, the National Institute of Mental Health (NIMH) made significant policy contributions to the national effort to expand the recruitment and use of members of racial and ethnic minority groups among both students and faculty in social work education programs.[4]

This article will examine some of the forces behind the establishment of these federally funded programs and will analyze the implementation of one program designed to rectify the underrepresentation of minority graduate students at four schools of social work in Texas. An alternative model of implementation will then be presented.

## Background

Prior to 1968, two graduate schools of social work—the School of Social Work at the University of Texas at Austin and the Worden

School of Social Service at Our Lady of the Lake University of San Antonio—had been in operation for nineteen years in the state of Texas. During this period, a total of 761 students were graduated from these schools: 138 were minority students. Of these, 54, or 7.1 percent, were black, and 84, or 11 percent, were Mexican American.[5]

This disproportionately low enrollment of minority students may be partially explained by the history of institutional racism in the Texas educational system. Other reasons for this phenomenon have been suggested at various times. They are the following: (1) increasing opportunities for minorities in professional fields other than social work, (2) the comparatively low status of social work as a profession, (3) the tendency of minorities to perceive social work and social welfare as some form of social control, and (4) the absence of a conscious effort by schools of social work to recruit minority students aggressively.

Even lower than minority student enrollment in schools of social work was the number of faculty members representing ethnic and racial minorities in Texas. This reflected a national pattern. Several policy factors were to influence this situation. Chief among these were actions by the federal government that were part of its attempt to bring about changes in nationwide discriminatory practices.

Prior to 1976, NIMH had voluntarily assumed the responsibility of rectifying injustices that stemmed from discrimination. In the late sixties the Social Work Manpower Training Branch of NIMH was mandated to fund programs to train minorities in schools of social work. However, pressure against discrimination increased in the seventies, as civil rights legislation and regulations pertaining to integration and affirmative action in institutions receiving federal funds were applied to schools of social work. Specifically, universities and colleges with federal grants were required to comply with Executive Order 11246 and its implementing regulations or risk litigation or the loss of federal funds.[6] In addition, Title VI of the Civil Rights Act of 1964 and other legislation led the way to the 1976 regulations of the Office of Civil Rights of the U.S. Department of Health, Education, and Welfare, which required programs that previously discriminated against persons on the grounds of race, color, or national origin to take affirmative action to overcome the effects of prior discrimination.

Another important influence in changing policy was CSWE, which formulates standards for social work education and evaluates schools of social work in accordance with these standards. The accrediting body for professional education in social work, CSWE derives its authority from the National Commission on Accrediting.

As a result of federal regulations and demands from minority constituents, CSWE's Commission on Accreditation emphasized the need for special attention to minorities in its 1971 publication on standards for accreditation. Section 1234 of the standards stated that "a school must conduct its program without discrimination on the basis of race, color, creed, ethnic origin, age or sex. This principle applies to the selection of students, classroom and field instructors, and other staff, and to all aspects of the organization and program of the school."[7] In addition, section 1234A went on to state that "a school is expected to demonstrate the special efforts it is making to enrich its program by providing racial and cultural diversity in its student body, faculty, and staff."[8]

These standards provided the cornerstone for the minority struggle in social work education. Policy had been established; now the policy implementation process would begin. This article will examine the way in which schools of social work in one state responded.

## Texas Consortium

In July 1970 a social work training project funded by the Social Work Training Branch of NIMH began operation. Officially called "Social Work Education for Minority Groups in Texas," the project came to be known as the Texas Minority Consortium. It involved the four graduate schools of social work in Texas: the Graduate School of Social Work, University of Texas at Austin; the School of Social Work, University of Texas at Arlington; the Worden School of Social Service at Our Lady of the Lake University; and the University of Houston's Graduate School of Social Work. The model involved three major elements: a social work professional was employed as a faculty member in each school to coordinate recruitment activities in the school and to develop curriculum content on minorities, federal funds were used to provide financial assistance to minority students recruited by the schools, and an advisory board was developed to provide input to the overall effort. Each of these three areas will be discussed and analyzed from a policy implementation perspective.

### Minority Recruiters

The University of Texas at Austin was the grantee in the project and assumed responsibility for its implementation and coordination. Each of the four recruiters was hired by the dean of the graduate school of social work at which he or she was to work. The recruiter at Austin served in the dual role of recruiter and director of the project.

In addition to their recruiting responsibilities, which consisted of traveling across the state to meet with interested minority group members at undergraduate schools and social service agencies, awarding NIMH stipends, identifying and securing funds for additional stipends and scholarships when the number of minority students exceeded the number of NIMH stipends, and providing supportive measures for students in order to retain them in schools, the recruiters assumed all responsibilities that come with faculty status. They were required to meet the project's objective of developing minority curriculum content for the respective schools.

The project provided only partial salaries for the director and the other recruiters. Consequently, each school had to supplement the salaries, in return for which the respective deans had the right to select and hire the recruiters. Thus, the recruiters were under the direction of two bosses, the dean and the director of the project, hired by one and paid by both. Because each boss demanded maximum production, the recruiters found that they had assumed two full-time jobs and had to split their allegiance. In order to survive, they had to coordinate their efforts within their own schools cautiously. Coordination is extremely difficult to accomplish in a university department that is composed of many entrepreneurs, especially in a system where tokenism is in effect.

Furthermore, the recruiters were operating in environments that had not been receptive to minority concerns. Although the schools of social work in Texas paid lip service to minority issues, the rhetoric heard in public forums did not translate into behavior. This was obvious from the low number of minority group members among faculty and students and from the lack in the curricula of content related to minorities. The recruiters were initially viewed as token figures who were nevertheless given the burden of full responsibility to rectify the injustices and deficiencies of the schools regarding minority issues.

This is not to say that the system was openly hostile or did not in principle share the concerns of minorities. Clues as to why the principal actors in this situation may have apparently agreed with the objectives of the project yet failed to facilitate its full implementation are provided by Pressman and Wildavsky, who noted that any one or all of the following reasons could account for the lack of response to the efforts of the recruiters by the overall system:

☐ Direct incompatibility with other commitments,

☐ No direct incompatibility, but a preference for other projects,

☐ Simultaneous commitment to other projects,

☐ Dependence on others who lacked a sense of urgency regarding the project,

☐ Differences of opinion on leadership and proper organizational roles,

☐ Legal and procedural differences,

☐ Agreement coupled with lack of power.[9]

These reasons may have influenced not only the host system, but the recruiters as well, who had to play multiple roles with few financial resources. As Pressman and Wildavsky commented, "The federal design was stirring, but those who drew it up did not adequately appreciate how great the difficulties of implementation could be."[10]

## Federal Funding

The consortium project was designed around the hypothesis that funds for minority stipends would increase the minority enrollment in the four schools of social work in Texas. The number of stipends varied from year to year during the ten-year period the program was in operation and fluctuated according to the level of funding. The maximum number of stipends awarded on a yearly basis was twenty-four, which were equally divided among the four schools. Consequently, the total statewide number of minority students who could have graduated with NIMH stipends over a ten-year period was two hundred and forty.

It was the intent of the policymakers that the recruiters work cooperatively with their respective deans and schools and with the recruiters and deans of the other schools. In an effort to support each other and to maintain territoriality, the recruiters functioned under an oral agreement (referred to as a "gentlemen's agreement," even though one of the recruiters was female) that they each would exert more effort in recruiting members of the minority group that was most prevalent in their region. There appears to have been a correlation between this strategy and the racial and ethnic makeup of the recruiters. That is, blacks are more predominant than Chicanos in Houston and Arlington, where black recruiters were hired and where larger percentages of black students were enrolled, and more Chicanos than blacks live in San Antonio and Austin, where recruiters who were Chicanos were hired and where a higher percentage of students who were recruited and admitted were Chicanos rather than blacks. It seemed that if each recruiter concentrated on his or her own group, the total number of students who were blacks or Chicanos would balance out on a statewide basis. Although this agreement appears to have been sound, the results were not balanced, a point that will be discussed later.

During the project, tensions developed within each school between the recruiters and the minority students who were recipients of stipends. Each recruiter believed that he or she was doing the best job possible under the circumstances, but the students thought that the recruiters were not recruiting enough people from the students' own reference group. There is no doubt that each of the recruiters was recruiting the minimum number of minority students for which stipends were available. But the project called for more. It was the intent of policy established for the project that the recruiters would generate additional funds for more stipends and recruit minority students who were not in need of financial assistance. The schools were supposed to commit themselves to hiring additional minority faculty. Recruiters were also supposed to develop minority content and integrate it into the total curriculum. At the end of the project phase, the respective schools were supposed to maintain the positions of the recruiters or assume their functions and generate funds for subsequent minority stipends. This was an enormous operation for one person to oversee.

The situation was aggravated by the fact that one of the schools was not recruiting at the same rate as the others. The problem was attributed to the recruiter, who was not actively recruiting. Because the project director had no real authority or control over the recruiters, he could only encourage the recruiter to do better. The NIMH program officer, who had helped formulate the project's policy, threatened to withdraw funds from the school in question. This situation was quite controversial. Withdrawing funds from one school would, in a sense, benefit the other three schools because the remaining funds would be divided among them. It did not seem fair, however, to deprive potential students of aid because a recruiter was inefficient. The issue created dissension within and among the schools, with the recruiters and minority students taking sides. One may speculate that in order to keep peace, NIMH decided to continue funding all four schools in keeping with the initial proposal. The following year, the recruiter in question was fired by the new dean at the school and was not replaced, because the dismissal occurred during the phase-out year of the project. This was one of several points in the implementation phase when control from the national level had to be exerted in order to maintain equilibrium at the state level.

## Advisory Board

The project's advisory board was initially composed of the deans of the four schools of social work, five social work professionals who were blacks and five who were Chicanos, a minority student from each school, and a nonminority representative of the state chapter of the National Association of Social Workers. Throughout the life of the project the board's composition remained essentially the same, except during the 1974-75 academic year, when it was expanded to include five American Indian professionals, and during the 1975-76 academic year, when student representation was increased to include one black and one Chicano or Chicana representative from each school.

Two or three meetings of the board were held each year and were rotated among the schools. With the assistance of the project's director, the recruiter at the host school assumed responsibility for planning and running the meeting. In theory, the advisory board could have served as the most effective means of coordinating the project, had it maintained the true nature of an advisory board and been able to provide input to a separate policymaking body. Instead, vested interests and power imbalances detracted from the board's primary commitment to the project's mission. In addition, the composition of the board may have affected its efficiency. The four deans held power singularly and collectively; the four recruiters had authority through the nature of their positions; and the other board members had varying influence in different realms. The conflicts inherent in this arrangement made the board an administrative monster and resulted in few democratic decisions being made.

The deans functioned individually in making decisions regarding their schools. The recruiters were directly responsible to their deans in their efforts to maintain their positions within their respective schools. The advisory board members attempted to represent the needs and demands of their respective communities, which, at times, functioned at cross-purposes. The needs of each school and corresponding community may or may not have been in tune with the goals and objectives of the consortium.

Perhaps the infrequency of the board's meetings contributed to the apparent lack of decision making on its part. In the absence of consistent and continuous communication among deans, recruiters, and advisory board members, decisions were sometimes made unilaterally.

## Outcomes and Impact

The minority consortium was in existence for a total of ten years. According to Pressman and Wildavsky, "a basic reason why programs survive is that they adapt themselves to their environment over a long period of time."[11] However, it is remarkable that the consortium survived as long as it did, in view of the fact that it never became integrated into its environment. The consortium was never viewed as part of the environment but merely as an appendage funded by NIMH. It might have been seen as a success if its mission, goals, and objectives had been integrated into the schools during its operation and if its goals had been incorporated into the social work programs after its phase-out period. This did not occur. Nevertheless, its success in meeting one of its goals

**Table 1.**

**Percentage of Chicanos in Graduating Classes, 1970-79**

| School | 1970 | 1971 | 1972 | 1973 | 1974 | 1975 | 1976 | 1977 | 1978 | 1979 |
|--------|------|------|------|------|------|------|------|------|------|------|
| Arlington | 5.1 | 5.7 | 4.5 | 4.1 | 2.2 | 3.2 | 2.1 | 2.4 | 4.5 | 4.1 |
| Austin | 5.7 | 6.4 | 13.6 | 9.4 | 11.0 | 20.0 | 18.2 | 6.3 | 10.0 | 12.3 |
| Houston | 5.9 | 7.6 | 12.0 | 5.8 | 8.0 | 13.0 | 16.0 | 9.0 | 8.0 | 8.0 |
| Worden | 8.7 | 10.3 | 21.0 | 25.0 | 21.0 | 24.0 | 29.0 | 22.0 | 28.0 | 32.0 |

is reflected in the number of minority students who were recruited, funded, retained, and graduated with a master's degree in social work over the course of the project.

The enrollment of blacks and Chicanos in the Texas schools of social work rose during the years of the project. It is estimated that in this period the consortium provided approximately 300 stipends. However, these stipends did not account for the dramatic increase in the number of minority students graduating. Whereas two schools had graduated 138 minority students in the nineteen years preceding the consortium, four schools graduated 1,205 minority students in the course of the project, which amounted to half that time.[12] Of the 1,205 graduates, 703 were Chicanos, and 498 were blacks. (This total does not include the few American Indians who also received NIMH stipends.) It can therefore be concluded that recruiting efforts far surpassed the actual provision of stipends and that the activities of the consortium and other minority stipend programs account for these figures.

As already indicated, the project's recruiters agreed to focus on the minority group most prevalent in their schools' area. Results show that the two recruiters (at Houston and Arlington) agreeing to recruit more blacks than Chicanos did so and that those (at Austin and Worden) agreeing to focus on recruiting Chicanos significantly met their objectives.

Tables 1 and 2 give the percentage of each group in the schools' graduating classes for the years in question. The first year shown, 1970, reflects the situation prior to the beginning of the project.[13]

The years 1975 and 1976 seem to have been significant in that the figures move in the direction of peaking in three out of the four schools. Overall, the University of Texas at Arlington appears to be the school with the least effective recruiting efforts, according to the figures presented. The University of Texas at Austin shows a consistently low enrollment of blacks and a higher but fluctuating rate for enrollment of Chicanos. The most striking results show soaring figures of enrollment

## Table 2.

## Percentage of Blacks in Graduating Classes, 1970-79

| School | 1970 | 1971 | 1972 | 1973 | 1974 | 1975 | 1976 | 1977 | 1978 | 1979 |
|---|---|---|---|---|---|---|---|---|---|---|
| Arlington | 6.5 | 8.2 | 9.0 | 13.0 | 10.2 | 4.8 | 3.6 | 5.3 | 6.2 | 6.2 |
| Austin | 4.1 | 4.6 | 2.8 | 4.7 | 4.5 | 5.1 | 3.3 | 3.1 | 2.3 | 4.0 |
| Houston | 17.0 | 22.0 | 21.0 | 22.0 | 17.3 | 21.4 | 21.0 | 12.0 | 16.4 | 14.0 |
| Worden | 6.9 | 9.0 | 8.2 | 4.7 | 5.6 | 5.8 | 6.7 | 5.6 | 7.0 | 7.0 |

among Chicanos at the Worden School. One can only guess about the factors that may have influenced this high enrollment in San Antonio and to what degree the consortium was responsible. Our Lady of the Lake University is a private Catholic university. Most of the students receive financial assistance from the school in order to meet the high cost of a private education. The consortium provided fewer than ten stipends per year. Consequently, one can speculate that the Worden School actively developed alternative financial resources.

Another factor that may have contributed to the rising enrollment among Chicanos in this school is that about 50 percent of the population of San Antonio are Chicanos. It is logical to suspect that the ethnic representation of the community is reflected in the school's enrollment. However, one may also speculate that the large numbers of faculty members who are Chicanos at the Worden School and that the mission of the school, which is to focus the curriculum on Chicanos, may be strong variables in attracting students.

Because of the Worden School's major contribution to the state's activities in the recruitment of Chicanos, the overall effort appears to have been quite significant. The Worden School graduated a total of 378 Chicanos in a ten-year period—54 percent of the total number of graduates who were Chicanos.

The agreement by which each recruiter made efforts to recruit the minorities most highly represented in his or her school's community worked out, but blacks and Chicanos were not recruited in equal numbers. The effects of the agreement are difficult to forecast. Will the recruitment of one particular minority above another create an imbalance in the number of professionals in that group? Will minority communities be underserved by professionals of their group? Only time will tell.

It is also difficult to analyze the impact of the consortium in terms other than those of numerical outcomes. Whether or not it met its other goals may have had more to do with the fact that aspirations were set too high than with individual failures.[14] The schools of social work in Texas were so deficient in every respect regarding minorities that the goals of the consortium were not feasible in several areas. Also, the consortium did not generate the interest or the commitment necessary from the schools. They never contributed resources to hire additional minority faculty or gave the assistance necessary to develop minority curriculum content. Without their assistance, it was impossible for the consortium to meet its objectives.

# Recommendations

It is the contention of the author that, had the initial project proposal contained a significantly different model of administration and program implementation, some of the political and organizational problems that impeded efficiency and effectiveness would have been brought under control, if not avoided. The model about to be suggested might have led to the same results, everything else being equal. On the other hand, it might have helped avert some of the crises that threatened the life of the program. This model would make changes in the areas of administrative structure, program, and evaluation.

## Administrative Structure

The consortium would have been set up as an autonomous, self-governing unit responsible for policy development and program implementation in cooperation with the funding source, the schools of social work, and the rest of the task environment. The organizational principle operating here is Fayol's "unity of command," which states that no one can serve two masters.[15] Rather than any one school having been designated grantee, the consortium, as a nonprofit corporation, would have been awarded the grant and concomitant authority and responsibilities.

As a nonprofit corporation, the consortium would have been governed by a board of directors made up of minority community leaders, professionals, and alumni of each of the schools. The initial board could have been selected by the funding source in consultation with the schools and representatives of these groups. The board would have been kept at a manageable size of from fifteen to twenty-one members and would have operated under a set of bylaws that dictated the periodic rotation of one-third of its members. This would have ensured the board's viability, avoided insularity, and facilitated continuity in policymaking.

The board of directors would have been responsible for hiring the consortium's administrator, who, in turn, would have recruited and hired one support staff member and one recruiter for each of the four schools. Thus, an expanded staff would have been responsible for carrying out the policies of the board, meeting federal guidelines, and implementing the program.

Finally, a linkage system would have been established to assure cooperation, coordination, and communication among the consortium and the four schools. One way of doing this would have been to develop contractual agreements with the schools, outlining the relationship between them and the consortium. In addition, an advisory council composed of the deans, minority students, and admissions staff from the four schools could have been set up to assist the consortium.

## Program

A recruiter would have been assigned to and housed in each of the schools for the purpose of recruiting for that school. The recruiter would have been responsible for recruiting blacks and Chicanos in equal numbers. The consortium's administrator would have had the responsibility for seeing that a balance in the recruitment effort was maintained. The state would have been divided into four geographic areas, with each recruiter assigned to his or her own recruitment turf.

In order to reach the objective of developing curriculum content related to minorities, the schools would have had to give the recruiters the faculty status of assistant professor, at the least. A minimal teaching load of one class could have been assigned to allow recruiters to introduce minority content. Each recruiter also would have been responsible for consulting with other faculty in efforts to develop and implement minority content. Moreover, the staff of the consortium would have assumed responsibility for the development of a model curriculum package to be presented to all schools for incorporation into their overall curriculum.

Selection of students for stipends would have been the responsibility of the consortium, which would have worked in consultation with admissions personnel. The admission of students would have been the responsibility of each school, to be carried out in consultation with the assigned recruiter and the consortium's director. To facilitate the achievement of the program's objectives regarding minority faculty, the consortium's staff could also have assumed the responsibility for helping schools identify, recruit, and hire minority faculty.

## Evaluation

An evaluation component would have been developed to assess the impact of the program in relation to its stated objectives. Evaluation would not have focused solely on numbers of students recruited, admitted, and graduated; information about where students went to work after graduation and the impact they had on agency services would also have been compiled. This may be too ambitious a recommendation, but it seems appropriate in view of the policy assumptions and objectives that led to the birth of the consortium.

These recommendations suggest an alternative model for the consortium that would provide it with a greater degree of freedom from the schools. This model would also allow for a more equal balance of power by differentiating the roles and responsibilities of all the actors. If such policy changes could have been made, perhaps the implementation process could have been easier. This suggestion is in accordance with the thoughts of Pressman and Wildavsky, who state that the great problem is to make the difficulties of implementation a part of the initial formulation of policy.[16]

# Conclusion

This article has attempted to provide a detailed description of the policy implementation process followed by the Texas Minority Consortium. An alternative model has been provided that incorporates modifications of the initial consortium proposal. The original consortium is gone, but perhaps new policies can be developed to help realize its mission and goals. We cannot cease to remind schools of social work that the minority struggle continues and that efforts will persist until the needs of all minorities are met by the profession born for this very purpose.

## Notes and References

1. Lillian Ripple, *The Quality and Structure of Social Work Education: A Report* (New York: Council on Social Work Education, 1974).

2. Ibid.

3. Rosalie Jo Mollenhauer, "A Study to Identify the Predictors of Minority Enrollment Success in Master Degree Social Work Programs," p. 1. Unpublished Ph.D. thesis, University of Texas at Austin, 1976.

4. Ripple, op. cit., p. 7.

5. Librado de Hoyos, *Decade in Minority Recruitment in Social Work Education in Texas* (San Antonio, Tex.: Our Lady of the Lake University, August 1980), p. 38.

6. See Executive Order 11246, as amended by Executive Order 11375 and 11478, in *Higher Education Guidelines* (Washington, D.C.: U.S. Department of Health, Education, & Welfare, October 1, 1972).

7. *Manual of Accrediting Standards for Graduate and Professional Schools of Social Work* (New York: Council on Social Work Education, April 1971).

8. Ibid., p. 6.

9. Jeffrey L. Pressman and Aaron Wildavsky, *Implementation* (Berkeley: University of California Press, 1973), pp. 99-102.

10. Ibid., p. 134.

11. Ibid., p. 116.

12. See De Hoyos, op. cit., pp. 56-71.

13. More detailed figures are available from the author; 1979 was the last year for which complete figures were available.

14. Pressman and Wildavsky, op. cit., chapter 22.

15. Henri Fayol, *General and Administrative Management* (London, England: Sir Isaac Pitman & Sons, 1971).

16. Pressman and Wildavsky, op. cit., p. 143.

# Glossary of Spanish Words and Phrases

**a Dios orando (*or* rogando) y con el mazo dando*** – praying to God and pounding with a mallet; an expression indicating the need for simultaneous prayer and action.

**Anglo** – white person of non-Hispanic extraction living in the United States.

**asustado(a)** – frightened; sometimes used to describe someone who feels as though his or her spirit has left the body.

**barrio** – area in which Spanish-speaking people live within a city; sometimes used interchangeably with "ghetto."

**cada cabeza es un mundo** – literally, each head is a world; an expression acknowledging the individuality of each person.

**Chicano(a)** – person of Mexican American extraction; a term used for self-definition and to reflect an ideological perspective that affirms the culture and heritage of Mexican Americans.

**confianza** – trust or bonding.

**conocimiento** – understanding or knowledge.

**conscientización** – educational method and philosophy used widely in Third World countries to teach literacy and create an awareness of repressive conditions; Spanish translation of the Portuguese *conscientizacao*.

**consejos** – advice or wise counsel; when used in a therapeutic setting, the term also means sharing.

**consideración** – consideration.

**cortesía** – courtesy.

**curandero(a)** – native spiritual and herbal healer.

**de** - of, from, or about.

**de acuerdo con otro** – in agreement with another.

**descarado(a)** – literally, a person without face; a shameless person.

**dirección** – direction or definite guidance.

**el** – the; masculine form of the word.

**espíritu** – spirit or soul.

**esta muchacha es una mortificación; parece que nos pucieron un maleficio** – this girl is a mortification; it seems as though we have been cursed.

**estar de acuerdo** – to be in accord.

**familia** – family.

**hacienda** – large, self-sufficient ranch.

**hombre** – man.

**la** – the; feminine form of the word.

**la borrachera de mi hijo es pura mortificación** – my son's drinking is pure mortification.

**la paciencia retira la mortificación** – patience alleviates mortification.

**Latino(a)** – person born in Latin America or of Latin American descent, who acknowledges Hispanic roots and lives in the United States.

**mal** - an evil or illness.

**maldicido(a)** - a person who has been cursed.

**maldición** - a curse.

**maleficio** - an evil or a malevolence.

* All terms listed are subject to local and regional variation.

**Mexicano(a)** – Mexican person living either in the United States or in Mexico; a term usually applied to a resident alien who feels a strong tie to Mexico.

**mortificación** – mortification.

**mortificado(a)** – tormented.

**mortificar** – to mortify.

**mortificar el cuerpo** – to punish or flagellate the body as a form of religious penance.

**movidas** – interactional strategies using common sense.

**orgullo** – pride.

**pasé tantas vergüenzas y mortificaciónes que me quise morir** – I felt so ashamed and humiliated that I wanted to die.

**patrón** – ruling elder in a village.

**persona** – person.

**pesadilla** – nightmare.

**plática** – warm, friendly conversation.

**platicando se entienden las cosas** – by conversing, people can understand each other's situation.

**podemos sequir adelante; hemos visto que sí se puede** – we can continue forward and onward; we have seen that it can be done.

**Pueblos Viejos** – literally, Old Towns; towns settled by Mexican Americans in the southwest United States that became the birthplaces of many southwestern cities.

**Raza** – literally, race; used to refer to people from Spanish-speaking backgrounds, including Mexicans, Puerto Ricans, Latin Americans, and those from other Spanish-speaking countries, predominantly used by Mexicans in referring to themselves.

**respetado(a)** - respected.

**respeto** – respect.

**sin vergüenza** – literally, shameless; used to describe someone lacking in self-respect and respect for others and engaging in objectionable behavior.

**sí se puede** – yes it can be done.

**sociedades de mutua protección** – mutual aid societies; a term referring to burial societies that also provided social support to their members.

**Tejano(a)** – person living in Texas.

**triste** – sad.

**tú** – you; the form of "you" used to address people who are younger than oneself or whom one knows well or to address someone in a familiar or intimate way.

**un(o)** or **(a)** – a; an.

**usted** – you; the formal form of "you" used to address people with whom one is not familiar or to show respect, usually for rank or age.

**vamos a platicar** - let's talk.

**vergüenza** – shame; this term may also refer to a person's sense of responsibility and social reputation and to a belief that individual success must not violate communal goals and solidarity.

**yo tengo mortificaciónes; tu tienes mortificaciónes; todos tenemos mortificaciónes** - I have mortifications; you have mortifications; we all have mortifications.